ENDORSEMENTS FOR CONFIDENT FAITH

In *Confident Faith*, my friend and fellow evangelist, Dr. Larry Brice, has written a significant and timely book. It is an honest, intelligent, and powerful response to the prominent secular atheists of our time. It is eloquent, scholarly and accessible. It has strong appeal to believers and non-believers alike. Dr. Brice's depth of knowledge and his passionate, committed and confident faith in the Lord Jesus Christ are evident throughout. Congratulations, Dr. Brice!

—*John Wesley White, D.Phil,*
associate evangelist with Billy Graham

Larry Brice focuses on the single most important problem for the defense of Christian faith today: the idea that faith is "belief without evidence." Historically, that's nonsense. Christian martyrs died because they refused to deny what they had personally witnessed. Under the spell of this seductive nonsense, many Christians today respond to the relentless attacks of secular atheists by saying, "I am entitled to my cozy little beliefs!" Dr. Brice shows why we shouldn't do that, why we don't need to, and how to use evidence when defending the faith.

—*Denyse O'Leary, science journalist & bestselling author of*
By Design Or By Chance; The Spiritual Brain; *and*
What are Newton's Laws of Motion?

My Presbyterian colleague, Dr. Larry Brice, has a passion not only to share his Christian faith, but to convince those who remain suspicious or even skeptical about faith matters. His new book, *Confident Faith*, provides a thoughtful, popular guide to the sort of evidence from nature, Bible, and theological reflection that suggest that faith in God makes sense. Dr. Brice has read widely; but, what strikes the reader most is his own enthusiastic Christian faith that has been truly tested and tried during his life. I commend Dr. Brice's new book, with the hope that it will encourage doubting Christians, and help make new ones.

—*Clyde Ervine, PhD, senior minister,*
Central Presbyterian Church, Hamilton, Ontario

Larry Brice has made an impact worldwide through his teaching, writing and television ministry. His new book is grounded in his solid academic training and his walk of faith as an evangelist for Jesus Christ.

—*James A. Beverley, PhD, professor of Christian*
thought & ethics, Tyndale Seminary, Toronto

In his book, *Confident Faith*, Dr. Brice seeks to set out a dialogue between an experiential knowledge of God and what he calls, quoting St. Paul, "true and rational words." He seeks not only to allow theology to speak with its own "scientific methodology"—the most significant for him being that of his mentor, T.F. Torrance—but also to do so without neglecting knowledge of God that comes from the natural world. It is an ambitious project. Here, presented through the personal experiences of the author, honestly and humbly shared, and those of others he has encountered along the way, a depth of faith, a confident faith, is presented that has the potential in its own right to convince the reader of the power of "developing a relationship with God."

—*J. Dorcas Gordon, M.Div, Th.D., Th.M.,*
principal and professor of biblical interpretation
and preaching, Knox College, University of Toronto

CONFIDENT FAITH

CONFIDENT FAITH

In a World That Wants to Believe

DR. LAWRENCE BRICE

Deep River BOOKS

Sisters, Oregon

CONFIDENT FAITH
In a World That Wants to Believe
© 2012 by Dr. Lawrence Brice

Unless otherwise marked, all Scripture quotations are taken from the New Revised Standard Version Bible, copyright 1989, Division of Christian Education of the National Council of the Churches of Christ in the United States of America. Used by permission. All rights reserved.

Scripture quotations marked "KJV" are taken from The King James Version of the Bible.

Scripture quotations marked NIV are taken from the Holy Bible, New International Version®. NIV®. Copyright © 1973, 1978, 1984 by International Bible Society. Used by permission of Zondervan. All rights reserved.

Scripture quotations marked NASB are taken from the New American Standard Bible, © Copyright 1960, 1962, 1963, 1968, 1971, 1972, 1973, 1975, 1977, 1995 by The Lockman Foundation. Used by permission.

Scripture quotations marked "ESV" are taken from The Holy Bible, English Standard Version. Copyright © 2000; 2001 by Crossway Bibles, a division of Good News Publishers. Used by permission. All rights reserved.

Published by Deep River Books
Sisters, Oregon
http://www.deepriverbooks.com

ISBN 13: 9781937756093
ISBN 10: 1937756092
Library of Congress Control Number: 2012934448

Printed in the USA

Interior design: Juanita Dix • www.designjd.net
Cover designer: Henry Miersma

This book is dedicated to the terrific women in my life:
my talented wife, Karen,
Alena and Erika, my two exuberant daughters,
my loving sisters, Marilyn and Rosemary,
and sister-in-law Glenda,
and to the other supportive man in here,
my brother-in-law, Mike.
My world starts every day and continues to run because of all of you!

Acknowledgments

A number of very special people have helped with the publication of this book.

I benefited greatly from my literary agent, Kimberly Shumate, who made the first suggestions to help prepare the book for a mass market.

Bill Carmichael of Deep River Books was the first publisher to take an interest in my manuscript. His further encouragement led me to enter a large competition with Deep River for best manuscript, in which I was a finalist and won an Award of Merit. Thanks for not giving up on me, Bill.

In fact, all those with him at Deep River Books are exceptional. Special thanks to managing editor Lacey Hanes Ogle, and to the design department for their engaging concept for the cover. Also, I give my deepest gratitude for the terrific help, advice, and hard work from my editor, Rachel Starr Thomson. You guys are all beyond belief!

Thanks also for your advice, Rev. Sandy Young. You read the first draft and greatly supported it for publication. Special thanks to my lawyer nephews, Graydon Ebert and Stephen Orr, and to Stephen's wife, Tina Lee, a PhD student at the University of Toronto, who all read the first draft of the manuscript. You guys gave me my first, unfettered feel for my public. Thanks. Also, thanks to my sister Marilyn, and to the Rev. Samir Aboukeer, for reading the manuscript and continuing your support for me and the gospel.

To Principal Dorcas Gordon, churchman Dr. Clyde Ervine, and bestselling author Denyse O'Leary, my grateful thanks; also, to internationally recognized author and apologist, Prof. James Beverley, and to my friend and associate evangelist with Billy Graham, Dr. John Wesley White—to all of you, my very special thanks for writing your endorsements.

From beginning to end, the emotional and creative continuum for my life comes from my supportive wife, Karen, whom I deeply love. I always thrive from our enjoyable companionship and conversations together!

Now, under all my acknowledgments, comes the foremost thanks to God the Father, God the Son, and God the Holy Spirit, who inspires and sustains every ministry he calls me to pursue. I humbly give Gloria Deo!

Table of Contents

Introduction

The Facts or a Leap of Faith? Starting with the World Around Us

A favorite television program with many viewers, including my wife, Karen, is *The View*, a talk show starring Barbara Walters, Joy Behar, Elizabeth Hasselbeck, Whoopi Goldberg, and Sherri Shepherd. Recently, they discussed the topic of intelligent design: the meaningful, purposeful, and intelligent design in the natural world that many see as evidence for an Intelligent Designer—that is, evidence for God.

The youngest member on the show, Elizabeth Hasselbeck, touched off a heated exchange when she commented:

> If I found Michaelangelo's statue of David without knowing who made it, I would see the sculptured hands and feet, the muscular arms and legs, and from this design I would know that it didn't come from the blind laws of nature working by chance—but from an artist with intelligence, purpose, and mind.

"In the same way," she said, "all the design we see in the natural world makes us conclude that there is a God of design and intellect."

Next was a comment from Joy Behar—really a classic observation that so many people make today, even people who already strongly believe in God.

"What do you mean this proves the existence of God?" Joy questioned. "God is only a matter of faith for those who want to believe, because there is not a scintilla of evidence in the world for the existence of God!"[1]

This conversation makes really good television and reflects the current debate on whether faith is based on real, factual evidence in nature and history or whether faith is a matter only of subjective feelings, intuitions, and longed-for hopes.

Historically over the last one hundred and fifty years and for many people today, especially as manifested in the television and print media, faith is no longer connected to any concrete, tangible evidence in the real world, but is simply something, however laudable, based on the personal thoughts and feelings in believers' lives. This vague idea of faith received its most classic and lasting expression in the nineteenth-century Danish philosopher Søren Kierkegaard. Writing *Philosophical Fragments*[2] in 1844, Kierkegaard was no longer able to find any evidence for God in the natural world, since the concept of "natural theology" (knowledge of God's existence revealed in the world of nature) had been destroyed by eighteenth-century Enlightenment philosophers like Immanuel Kant and David Hume. So if there is no evidence or proof for God in the natural world, how does the believer move from our existence in this world to God's existence above?

In answer, Kierkegaard coined the expression that what needed to be done was for the believer to make "a leap of faith." The words were to be to his lasting fame, but to the tragic peril of much later theology.

This idea still completely dominates much popular thought about God in the Western world. Critics of Christianity, along with many believers, think that's how the believer arrives at faith in God—not so much from any evidence in the natural world, but as a mental "leap" from the natural, physical world to faith in an almighty God *above* the natural world. Obviously, this is the view expressed by Joy Behar and a vast number of others, especially in the mass media.

NOT A TEXTBOOK—A TESTIMONY

If you haven't given up on finding faith in God and want some very good reasons to believe, then this is the book for you. It will seek to demonstrate that reliable, convincing evidence for the existence of God can be found: first, Enlightenment philosophers notwithstanding, in our personal experience of the natural world all around us; second, in the most reliable recorded religious history; and third, in the storms we face in life. Here I will rely on my own story: I have seen life at its worst and have had the courage to come back with the help of an almighty God who has proven to be truly there.

However, please note this is more than just a textbook arguing only from philosophy, history, and theology for a rational faith in God. This book will deal with many of these topics, but not to engage directly with every argument raised in the fierce attack by atheistic writers such as Christopher Hitchens, Sam Harris, biologist Richard Dawkins, or mathematician John Allen Paulos, the latter in his recent book, *Irreligion: A Mathematician Explains Why the Arguments for God Just Don't Add Up*.[3] It will, however, be necessary to answer a number of their main objections to Christian theism in order to make a convincing case for the existence of God.

Recently, massive interest in the question of whether God exists has erupted, largely thanks to the books by these zealous atheists. For example, when I went to my local branch of the Toronto Lending Library to borrow Dawkins's book *The God Delusion*, I was told that the book wasn't yet in the system. When asked if I would like to make a reservation for it, I asked how many reservations were ahead of me. The librarian looked the number up and replied, "About two thousand!"

A recent poll shows that atheism is the fastest growing (ir)religious movement in Canada. Thirty years ago, only 7 percent said they didn't believe "in any God," whereas in 2007 this poll revealed that atheism has leaped to 23 percent of the Canadian population![4] Many people, even in the church, are looking for answers to the questions about God. And these questioners want a rational and well-argued answer!

Faith and rational thought do not conflict with each other, but work best when brought together. Our knowledge of God is called *theology*, and it makes the most sense when studied with its own scientific methodology, such as we find in Thomas F. Torrance's momentous work, *Theological Science*.[5] This book received the highest religious award in the world, the Templeton Prize for Progress in Religion, in 1978. It is acclaimed for its reconstruction of rational science in the study of God, providing clarity and conviction in the study of orthodox Christianity. Thomas F. Torrance, my former professor, writes that God can be studied using rational, scientific methods, but only in ways completely appropriate to the subject matter—which means that we can know God only out of God's self-disclosure to us. I will show in this book that God discloses his glory both in natural revelation in nature, and in the special revelation and history recorded in the Holy Bible.

While I do not have space to answer the atheists on every one of their points, I will refer to the most important themes they have raised. My intention is to put a completely human face to all these themes by showing how the philosophical and theological arguments for God have actually impacted and changed my own life.

We will deal with controversial issues, but through the lens of a journal—really an odyssey of personal experience—of how an intelligent believer has experienced these academic issues directly and powerfully in personal life.

We will start with knowledge of God from nature, studying the arguments for the existence of God from the natural world. This section will also share the author's personal journey from youthful atheism into believing in God as the First Cause of creation and the Intelligent Designer, and later into more mature theism.

Knowledge of God from the natural world has been called *natural theology*.

Much Protestant theology for the last seventy-five years has suffered from neglected and ignored natural theology,[6] although many Roman Catholic and Anglo-Catholic theologians[7] have not only used it extensively, but have been highly successful in reconstructing it into a potent intellectual force in presenting a rational faith in God.

It cannot be overstated that to neglect our knowledge of God from nature not only impoverishes our understanding, but can disconnect us from the most meaningful and powerful discourse we have in common with unbelievers, apart from the more important and indispensable task of witnessing to the revealed truth of God in the Christian Bible.

Part 1 will develop the evidence for God in nature as its First Cause and creation's Intelligent Designer. In Part 2, we will examine the Bible in some detail as the revealed history of almighty God entering our human world through the prophets, priests, and kings of the Old Testament, an interaction which finds its full consummation in the life, death, and resurrection of God's Son, Jesus Christ, in the New Testament. In each chapter, I will add a brief testimony that affirms the theological truths proven in my own life.

In Part 3, I will tell my story of falling from the heights of the world's greatest seminary into the depths of the deepest psychological pain, only to find God to be the "rock and refuge" under my feet in that pit, the one who always remained the firm foundation under me to help me get back on my feet and come again to God's fullness of life.

A passage in the Bible presents the rationale for this book. It appears in the story of the apostle Paul, the first century's greatest Christian advocate, when he appeared before Governor Festus and King Agrippa in a court case to defend himself for his volcanic ministry to the Gentiles and his fellow Jews. This scene is filled with intense drama because Paul's life was at stake. Paul explained to the king how his life had changed radically on the Damascus Road from persecuting Christians to actually becoming one of them. Paul not only defended himself, but took the opportunity to witness about his Lord Jesus Christ to his royal audience. The Bible tells this event best:

And as he was saying these things in his defense, Festus said with a loud voice, "Paul, you are out of your mind." But Paul said, "I am not out of my mind, most excellent Festus, but I am speaking *true and rational words*. For the king knows about these things and to him I speak boldly. For I am persuaded that none of these things has escaped his notice, for this has not been done in a corner. King Agrippa, do you believe the prophets? I know that you believe." And Agrippa said to Paul, "In a short time would you persuade me to be a Christian?" And Paul said, "Whether short or long, I would to God that not only you but also all who hear me this day might become such as I am—except for these chains." (Acts 26:24–29, ESV, emphasis mine)

Paul declared that he was speaking boldly in "true and rational words." Like Paul in his day at court, I want to present true and rational words about the Lord, a God whose creative hand is visible in our natural world and in our most reliable religious history.

The reader will find in each chapter both the intellectual information for God, and, in the pattern of Paul, an account of how I have proven the truth in personal experience. I hope the reader will find in this book the thoughts and experiences of an informed believer and will see with me the fingerprints of God throughout the natural world and in our best recorded human history, especially in the Christian Bible.

Now, discover for yourself the undeniable evidence for a confident faith in God.

PART 1

God in Nature

CHAPTER 1
From Maple Leaves
to the First Cause

So much current thinking on God is inadequate because many scholars do not begin with any firsthand experiences of God—or is even more desperately impoverished because of an absence of any good knowledge of God from the natural world.

How absolutely essential for the Christian to start theology with arguments from personal experience and evidence for God from the natural world! Such an approach can and will help people seeking for God to start with the right assumptions, expecting to prove the living God and not simply seeking to disprove something they haven't already found.

As an undergraduate at the University of Toronto, I remember an English doctoral student friend returning from a lecture by one of the world's leading English theorists, Northrup Frye. My friend made this observation: "Why is it that evangelical Christians always try to drag people closer and closer to the center of what they believe about God? It's like a centrifuge sucking people into the center of their opinions!" And then he added, "Professor Frye suggested in his lecture that seekers after the truth of God try to kill off all the false gods they can, and whatever God is left is the true God."[8]

This is negative theology with a major negative assumption: that one must approach the question of God's existence by trying to disprove it. If one approaches the Scriptures with this negative unbelief, trying to "kill off" the theological claims and miracles, it will result in an entirely different theology from what the Bible is clearly offering. Much current theology is bogged down in this miasma, with little hope of finding any reliable knowledge of God.

If there is any true, authentic, and accurate information about God, then how, we ask, do we start to find it?

It all starts with our knowledge of God from personal experience and the natural world—from the common physical reality we share with the people of all religions or of no religion at all. In fact, we can see everywhere that our natural world is filled with clues for God.

When you begin the study of anything, you must start with a hypothesis assuming what you hope to find. This chapter is meant to open the mind in a positive way, so instead of trying to *disprove* the existence of God, you can come expecting that something might actually be there. After all, this is exactly what the Bible says is the proper assumption for any seeker after truth: "For whoever would approach him must believe that he exists and that he rewards those who seek him" (Hebrews 11:6). Such a positive assumption, expecting to find God in our search, is also the experiment that Jesus invites us to make: "For everyone who asks receives, and everyone who searches finds, and for everyone who knocks, the door will be opened" (Matthew 7:8). Beginning the search for God with these positive assumptions will set up for the seeker a positive experience of God!

AN EARLY EXPERIENCE OF GOD FROM MAPLE TREES

In my early life as a young boy, I saw the world as an atheist despite having grown up in a committed Christian family. I realized I didn't believe in God when I was about ten or eleven years of age.

Every Sunday I would go with my father, who was the local postmaster, and my mother, a homemaker, and the rest of my family to St. Andrew's Presbyterian Church in Maple, Ontario, where we lived. At that time, Maple was a small village of about one thousand people just north of Toronto. I had lived there since I was five.

Maybe it was only to seek attention (being the second born in the family), but I remember as an eleven-year-old coming home after church and shouting at my mother, "I don't believe there is a God! God doesn't exist! I don't want to go back to that church anymore!"

We sang hymns in Sunday school with words like this:

God sees the little sparrow fall, it meets his tender view.
If God so loves the little birds, I know he loves me too.

I could see the little birds, but I just could not see God in my world!

But we did go back to church every weekend. That was what was expected in our family. Then came a huge surprise.

One Sunday morning in Sunday school, my teacher, Mrs. Bowman, the minister's wife, conducted a class on creation for the three boys in her class. It was October, and the maple trees that lined Keele Street going into Maple were scarlet red and sunburnt yellow. She pointed to one of these magnificent trees just outside the Sunday school room window and asked this question:

"Boys, where did that beautiful tree come from?"

I knew the answer, and my arm shot up: "From the seeds in the leaves when they fall to the earth on the ground."

"Boys," she continued, "where did the earth come from?"

Again, I thought I knew: "From when the sun and earth were formed," I answered from my very basic knowledge of public school science.

But she continued once again: "Boys, tell me where the earth and the sun come from."

Something happened to my mind when she asked this last question. This series of questions was really the rational evidence leading the mind toward belief in God. And it worked! I was absolutely amazed and exclaimed: "Mrs. Bowman, there is a God! He created it all at the beginning!"

As I spoke these words to Mrs. Bowman, God seemed to come right into the picture she had painted with her questions. It was almost as if a light had actually come on in my mind. I not only believed in God, but for the first time in my life, I experienced a Light—a glimmer of whatever it was that was out there.

When I got home, I excitedly told my family, "There really is a God! I know now, Mom and Dad, that there is a God!"

Later, in university, I learned that Mrs. Bowman had summarized a philosophical argument for the existence of God from sufficient causality, an argument that has been restored and restated in our own day by some philosophers and theologians with renewed vitality and convincing validity. It certainly worked for me as an adolescent with a searching and inquiring mind!

THE BEGINNING OF THE UNIVERSE:
ST. THOMAS AQUINAS'S FIVE WAYS

A medieval theologian by the name of Thomas Aquinas wrote very deep theological-philosophical books in which he offered "Five Ways" to prove the existence of God. This thirteenth-century thinker attempted to prove the existence of God in both his major works, *Summa Theologica* and *Summa Contra Gentiles*, which are extremely detailed and complicated.

Aquinas's Second Way to prove God was that of efficient *causality*. Many Catholic and Anglo-Catholic scholars have restored the proofs from Thomas Aquinas with great success. One of the greatest and most read, the late E.L. Mascall, former Professor of Historical Theology in the University of London (England), has written extensively on the traditional "proofs" for the existence of God, transforming what once were seen as logical proofs to what are now presented as existential arguments for the existence of God. For more detail, I refer you to Eric Mascall's brief summary of Aquinas's Second Way in the footnote.[9] Though Aquinas's other "Ways" are also worthwhile, here we will consider only his Second Way to prove God as the First Cause of the universe.[10]

Thomas Aquinas's Second Way demonstrates that nothing that we know in the universe has created itself. And the universe itself is not eternal, but has a beginning in time. How then did everything happen to come into existence if things don't make themselves and haven't existed eternally? The universe requires a First Cause, a Creator, who is different from created things in being great enough to account for itself and in being the First Cause of all created things. Having existed before temporal, created things, the First Cause can also be seen to have eternal existence. And this is what we mean by God.

There are five clear steps for proving God as the First Cause of the origin of the universe. If you thoughtfully take these steps with me, you will discover why it is completely rational to believe in God the Creator!

The first step is to accept as legitimate the terms *cause* and *effect*. Thomas Aquinas's argument moves from the finite world of cause and effect to what causes them all, the First Cause, God.

What then do these words mean? Basically cause and effect means that one thing makes another thing happen. The concept of cause and effect is highly useful in all our popular culture and news reporting. We all know the catastrophic damage that Hurricane Katrina caused in New Orleans in the USA. The hurricane was the terrible *cause* of the damage, which had a devastating *effect* upon the levies and homes there. Although some scientists and philosophers may not be able to nail down an exact definition, we all have a clear sense of what is meant by cause and effect. These terms must be accepted as meaningful as a first step.

We cannot stress enough that we start this argument by looking carefully at *the physical world around us*. Only when we clearly and unmistakably know the physical, finite world, where everything happens by cause and effect, can we start to see the truth of this demonstration of God.

Secondly, if we keep our eyes on real, existing things in the universe, we will not think that the Second Way is a blind thought existing solely within the mind. During the European Enlightenment of the eighteenth century, especially in the philosophy of Immanuel Kant, the argument from causality was too often dismissed as meaningless because Kant and others after him thought this argument was pure logic only, existing only in our minds with nothing to do with the real existing world outside our minds.[11]

Today, many atheistic philosophers echo Kant in saying this argument for God has nothing to do with real things but is only abstract logic, not pointing to anything you can experience at the end. "It's like saying that 1 + 1 = 2," they argue. You can see the logic of this mathematical term, but just to look at it and agree that it's true never tells you anything at all about the "real" world we know from our senses.[12]

But perhaps it is the philosophers who are not saying anything "real" here. In my childhood experience of God as the First Cause, Mrs. Bowman didn't offer us abstract logic like a mathematical term, but pointed out the real features of the existing maple trees. And as she went along from the trees to the earth, and then from the earth to the solar system, and finally to the First Cause at the beginning of this real universe, I experienced something of the Creator that led to my first discovery of whatever it was that was there. She led me in rational steps, moving reasonably from the existing observable world to the Existence that began it. Because I could know "existence" in the natural world, I could follow her to "Existence" in the spiritual world! These arguments are not at all only matters of logic and pure reason, as Kant and others declared, but are fully embedded in the structure of the physical universe linked to its creative First Cause!

Thirdly, nothing in the world we see around us causes itself to exist, but only exists as having been caused by something else. Nothing in the observable world has ever been able to create itself. For example, the Windows operating system I used in writing this book was caused by Microsoft. Microsoft was caused by Bill Gates and a plethora of other talented people. The *cause* of Microsoft has resulted in the *effect* of a highly usable computer technology which is used around the world. We clearly observe that nothing in the digital world has created itself. In the same way, every existing thing in the universe has been caused by something else. The universe itself is an unimaginable series of effects resulting from preexisting causes. We have never had a finite effect without a preexisting cause. Nothing we observe in the physical universe is self-caused—at anytime, anywhere, under any conditions! If the physical universe *began* with the big bang ten billion years ago, as many astronomers believe, then what created the finite cosmos cannot *itself* be anything finite, because we know that finite things never cause themselves to exist. Before things begin to exist, there must be a First Cause different from all created things in being great and capable enough to account for its own self-existence. This is what we call God.

Even if someone says that only something created and finite existed before and caused the big bang, we still have the same problem, because finite things are not capable of creating themselves. At some point before the big bang, if finite, created things existed, they could not have caused themselves to exist—we know from observation of the physical world that this is impossible. Finite existing things never are able to make themselves, so even if finite things preexisted the big bang, we keep going back until we reach Something of a completely different order and level of reality than the finite created world—something completely different, which alone must be great enough to account for its own reality. Being different from everything made by something else, and not being finite itself, we call this the *Infinite*. And this is what we mean by God.

Fourthly, this series of causes and effects does not go back forever. The series of effects created by causes is not without a beginning. How do we know this?

We must borrow here from the science of astronomy, which tells us from the best of their most widely accepted theories that the universe had a finite beginning about ten to fifteen billion years ago, caused by a massive explosion popularly called "the big bang" which began all the mass and energy of the entire cosmos. Not only that, but many astronomers believe that the universe is dying and will have a finite end.[13] All the mass and energy brought into being at the beginning when the stars were created is burning out and is nonrenewable. Astronomers say that at some future date over a vast period of time, the universe itself will be dead, without light or life. Obviously, if the universe will end in time, it has a limited lifetime and is therefore temporal. It can only have had a beginning in time as well; it cannot be eternal. Thus, the entire unimaginable series of effects with their causes is temporal and not eternal.

Fifth, what do we know about the First Cause that existed before the big bang? This is where some scientists stop their thinking, claiming that there is nothing we can know about what caused the big bang. These scientists park their thinking at this door, seeing nothing before creation, being unable to measure anything from before time began.

But we do know some things about this! From Newtonian physics, we know the law that "every action has an equal and opposite reaction." If the brand-new universe was the reaction, then there was a Cause sufficiently great to create it!

This First Cause had to be *huge* to result in our universe coming forth in the tiniest fraction of a second. In fact, considering the entire mass and energy of the cosmos, the First Cause must be almighty, probably far greater than all of creation itself, powerful beyond any imagining. Just keep your eyes on the physical universe to glimpse the magnitude of God's creative power. Hence we *do* know that what existed before the universe existed was/is hugely powerful; otherwise, it could not have resulted in what we observe in the cosmos. "Every action causes an equal and opposite reaction." Thus we do know the First Cause to be almighty. This First Cause must be sufficiently great to account for the almost inconceivably vast magnitude of the universe created by it.

Additionally, the atheist is quite right to say that we can't "measure" or "see" this First Cause. But instead of concluding from this that *nothing Godlike exists*, as the atheist tragically concludes, these observations are two of *the very attributes of God*. God cannot be seen or measured because "God is Spirit" as Jesus said (John 4:24), and as such, "no one has ever seen God" (John 1:18).

THIS IS NOT A CLEVER TRICK!

At this point in the discussion you may want to think about the above demonstration and process what has been said. This proof for God is not a trick by Christian theologians. Look at the world of cause and effect yourself, and observe the connection of the physical universe with its finite effects resting on and completely connected to the First Cause.

Atheist John Allen Paulos, in his book, *Irreligion: A Mathematician Explains Why the Arguments for God Just Don't Add Up*, says that these kinds of theological arguments are a "logical abracadabra" that "quickly leads to metaphysical bankruptcy."[14] Elsewhere, he calls them "a kind of verbal magic show."[15] These are terrific quips that look great in book reviews, but are of no help in answering or developing the issues involved.

Paulos, in much the same way as Dawkins, writes as a pop atheist attacking Christianity, and he gleefully surfs his way through the Second Way of Aquinas, tricking the reader with a superficial discussion that both obscures the real issues—with his rambling references to eastern religion, yoga, and quantum physics—and quits from any detailed, reasonable debate on the topic. The reader feels that Paulos is trying more to strike a mood in his book than deal intelligently with an argument—he resembles the man who preached a red-hot sermon that resulted in more heat than light.

Writing in *Canada's National Post*, celebrated columnist Robert Fulford reviewed *The God Delusion*, noting that Dawkins, a brilliant scientist and biologist at Oxford University in England, has a tragic flaw:

> Religion brings out the worst for Dawkins. It makes him awkward and sometimes silly. He considers religion stupid but doesn't realize that when he thinks about it he brings his IQ down a couple of dozen points. He becomes a preacher, and not a good one.[16]

Both Paulos and Dawkins appear to suffer from the same chronic theological deficiency when it comes to a rational study of Christian theism, despite the fact that Paulos sounds like an exceptional mathematician and can write an exciting, racy book! Ridicule and fuzzy thinking simply cannot substitute for rational argument, no matter what side of the fence they come from.

WHY SOME ATHEISTS WON'T AGREE

However, there remains a sensitive point to be made here about why the atheist, or maybe more appropriately the non-theist or agnostic, may still remain in doubt despite these carefully argued five points. Often, the atheist tries to counterargue every point, hoping to make the outcome a draw at the very least, and strongly wanting to believe that no one will win in this debate—certainly not the believer in God—thus removing humankind from any cogency for faith in God.

Even some of the greatest conservative Christian scholars, like Alister McGrath, professor of historical theology at Oxford University, writing in his recent book, *The Twilight of Atheism*, also tend to reject "proof" for God. McGrath observes:

> As Michael Polanyi insisted, there is always going to be an element of faith or trust, [i.e. going beyond what can be proven conclusively by the evidence] in the natu-

ral sciences, precisely because so much cannot be proven. And when it comes to the question of God, as we shall see, nothing can be proven at all—despite the interesting exaggeration of those who tell us otherwise, on both sides of the argument.[17]

So where are we, then, if neither the atheist nor even some of the greatest Christian theologians can accept the proof of this demonstration for God as the First Cause of the universe?

The answer lies in the real reason that the atheist cannot believe in God through the argument of cause and effect: it is because, from the very beginning, *they do not believe in God.* This may seem like a curious statement. Clearly speaking, can we or can we not prove the existence of God? Some atheists will always gravitate to "rational" counterarguments, no matter how disingenuous they are, so that conveniently nothing like God will need to exist for them. Also, they are strongly inclined not to believe in the proof for God because they have never seen, touched, or heard God in any previous experience before coming to this proof. They don't believe in God because they don't believe in God! This may seem like a tautology, but there is very great wisdom in this sentence. Hence their passion to sweep away this whole endeavor, often unfairly.

My thesis so far remains that everyone *can* know God from the created world. It certainly worked remarkably well for me, and I suspect for most other people as well. The Bible confirms belief in God from the natural world, as recorded in Psalm 19, or as St. Paul wrote in Romans 1:19–20:

> For what can be known about God is plain to them, because God has shown it to them. For ever since the creation of the world his eternal power and divine nature, invisible though they are, have been understood and seen through the things he has made. So they are without excuse.

But in quoting St. Paul, I have moved from the "philosophical" analysis of the natural world to the "theological" world of the Bible. Please note this significant shift, from philosophy to theology and history. The best evidence for encountering the existing God lies within the Bible, not only for the atheist, but for every honest seeker for the truth about deity. We anticipate here the middle section of this book, "God in History." There we will find that when we open the Bible and read about the life, death, and resurrection of Jesus Christ, we reach out and touch the very hem of the almighty Creator. Thus what may be missed in natural theology, which leaves some in unbelief, can be discovered in the positive theology of what God has actually said and done in the unveiling of himself in the history of the Bible.

Professor Tom Torrance made the point over and over again in his lectures that we "cannot steal knowledge from behind the back of God," from a study of God in nature, but only from the positive knowledge of God's self-disclosure in Jesus as recorded in the Bible.[18] But Tom once hinted to us students this significant hope for the seeker: that after we discover, *are redeemed*, and know with complete certainty the God positively disclosed in Jesus Christ, it is then that we will be able to go back and truly know and see the God revealed in the natural world as the First Cause and the Intelligent Designer. Those unmoved by natural theology may encounter God in the direct and comprehensible revelation God gives in positive theology.

Here rests the challenge to those who cannot yet believe: even if you cannot see God as the First Cause in our study of the natural world, read on to discover God in history, especially in the God revealed in the positive knowledge of Jesus, and then come back to the natural world. The wonderful opportunity to discover the living God, the hidden God of creation, as witnessed to in this book, can come from *either* our philosophical beginning or our theological ending!

In *The God Delusion*, Richard Dawkins does make one very good point as an atheist looking briefly at this argument for the

First Cause. He says that even if this argument is valid, we do not yet have anything that Christians proclaim as an all-wise, all-loving God who answers prayers for people on earth.[19] This is completely acceptable at this juncture in our search for God.

But at this point, please notice that *something very suspicious is happening here*. We possess a lingering suspicion, based on scientific reasoning, that Something like an almighty, powerful, self-existent Being lies behind the origin of the universe! What is more rational and reasonable than to look in our history for some contact with this creative Being? The search begins!

HASN'T EVERYONE ALREADY BELIEVED THIS?

Besides giving us an excellent starting point in the search for God, natural theology might also help us to explain the rise of the world's religions. Doesn't the concept of a powerful Being lie behind some of the most amazing structures of the ancient world, like the pyramids of Egypt, the rock monuments of Stonehenge, or the Mayan temples? These ruins of antiquity are founded upon a common belief that something awesome lay behind the observable universe.

Religion is one of the oldest features of civilization, and religious artifacts are found in many of the oldest archeological digs everywhere in the world. Nor is religion just a feature of the ancient world. Even today, in the most advanced countries of the world—like Canada, the United States, Northern Ireland, the UK, South Korea, and several European countries, religious belief is still very strong and active even among those people with the most brilliant minds! The Holy Bible has even been read on television by astronauts in space.

Early in the Christian and Hebrew Bible, in Psalm 19 the writer observes this fact of natural theology declaring the existence of God to the world:

The heavens are telling the glory of God and the firmament proclaims his handiwork. Day to day pours forth speech, and night to night declares knowledge. There is no speech, nor are there words; their voice is not heard; yet their voice goes out through all the earth and their words to the end of the world.

The theater of God's glory in nature silently declares God's existence to the whole world and can be most wonderfully heard from the glorious sight of the heavens above!

"Don't people everywhere already know about this God?" we may ask. The argument for a First Cause from nature isn't anything new or surprising—it really doesn't tell us anything the world doesn't already know. However, this argument gives us the indispensable logical proof, or rational explanation, of what we as human beings have experienced and known from the beginning of time.

While earning five university degrees—four from the University of Toronto and one from the University of Edinburgh in Scotland—I came to see that most people experience something like my experience of God in Sunday school that day, an experience I came to substantiate later in St. Thomas Aquinas's proof of God from causality.

For example, in the late 1980s, Dr. Billy Graham was sitting beside Raisa Gorbachev, the wife of the president of the former Soviet Union, when Russia was still officially an atheistic nation. He leaned over at the state dinner and asked her, "Do you believe in God, Mrs. Gorbachev?"

"Well," she measured her answer, "it had to start somewhere."

Here we see the very heart of our discussion. *I find that almost everyone, at some point in life, believes in a God who is the First Cause, but most people don't know why they believe this—they don't know how to explain it.* What I have tried to present in the above proof is the logical, articulate explanation for how we get to our belief in the First Cause—it's an attempt to explain why we already believe in God as we do! But there is a risk here too: without this proof from the natural revelation of God in creation, many don't know why *they* believe. Doubt can soon follow, and belief may weaken into a matter of "blind faith," leaving us holding onto Kierkegaard's empty "leap of faith" only. As our connection of God with the natural world diminishes, so too does faith!

There is a necessary lesson here for Protestants! We must overcome the disillusionment with natural theology that we have inherited from the skepticism of the eighteenth-century Enlightenment and from that great twentieth-century biblical thinker, Karl Barth, who so tragically ripped up and threw away any natural knowledge of God apart from God's positive revelation in Jesus Christ in Scripture.[20] We can help all unbelievers when we share a well-argued natural theology. Without a starting point of knowing God in the natural world, how can we ever talk about anything more that we discover in the religions of the world? Natural theology is the level ground on which we can all stand and talk together!

As Dawkins observed, we cannot assume belief in the full understanding of the Christian God at this point. What we have found is a huge, powerful, almighty, invisible, immeasurable First Cause that is completely complementary to the Christian idea of God. But is this all we can know? Can we only know that there is Something powerful out there? Indeed, we can discover much more than the mere understanding of God as the First Cause.

A far greater discovery lay ahead for me after Mrs. Bowman's Sunday school class. To my utter surprise, I found that this First Cause became *interactive. It responded to my words!*

CHAPTER 2
The Architect's Intelligent Design

After my early experience of God as the First Cause of the universe, the remainder of my public school days were spiritually uneventful—well, except for meeting an exceptional friend in grade six, Michael Spence, who later in life astounded us all by earning the Nobel Prize for Economics in 2002.

However, another personal God-event occurred in grade eight on a cold, crisp October night when I walked from our Victorian home under the glittering stars to the barn to feed my horse. At that time, there were no street lights in Maple to pollute the night sky with light, and the stars were brilliantly gleaming overhead. There I could see the thick disk of stars that formed our galaxy of the Milky Way, the constellations of the Big Dipper and Cassiopeia. I stopped and stared intently at this magnificent cosmic canopy overhead.

Then something I had not expected nor ever seen before happened. A shooting star cut a bright streak of light across the heavens.

It lasted only a few moments but caused a powerful emotional reaction in my heart. My thoughts went back to our local church, where our minister frequently proclaimed the existence of a personal God who answers prayer.

For several years, I had known that Something was out there. I could not imagine a universe that didn't have an all-powerful First Cause such as I had discovered in Sunday school. But that conviction didn't tell me anything about the Creator. That faith didn't tell me anything about my personal destiny, why I had been born, whether there was a heaven, or how to get there if there was life after death.

Really, mine was a faith common to many people—to almost everyone! It was basically a faith in "something there" which is relatively unknown. It was only a little more than philosophical atheism, in fact closer to agnosticism in that it was a faith that contained almost no information except an intelligent affirmation of divine existence.

Standing under the inscrutable stars, I wondered if I could experiment with this First Cause I believed in and that our minister was telling us about. I stared at the spot where the shooting star had appeared as I summoned up my courage and whispered these words:

"God if you are there, send another shooting star across the sky."

I waited three or four seconds, and then I said, "Do it now."

Within another second or two, a second shooting star shot across the heavens in the same location!

This terrified me! I thrust my head down and uttered under my breath to the First Cause, "Who am I, O God, to ask you to prove yourself to me? I am only a speck of dust on this earth, and I am so sorry to have asked this of you."

Many places in the Christian Bible say, "The fear of the Lord is the beginning of wisdom." At that moment, I had a great fear of what I had asked of God and what I thought God had done. But I had discovered something powerful on that starry night. Something had responded to the thoughts and words I sent up there. *Suddenly, my relationship with the First Cause was interactive!* There had been a personal, intelligent response to my words. There was a responsive mind. Words addressed to the First Cause like this are best understood as *prayer*, and here was proof of a living, interactive relationship with Something out there in this immediate response to my prayer!

We must answer at this point, "Does God do this kind of thing?" Many people have no experience of God's hand so directly active in their lives, even though they may believe in miracles. When I shared this manuscript with several relatives, one responded with this observation:

> Several times in your book you refer to witnessing events in nature as a direct proof of God answering your prayers. I recall you noting the shooting stars you came upon in eighth grade. I wonder how persuasive it is to make God appear as though he proves his own existence by actually answering children's prayers to send down another shooting star when it conveniences them, as though God operates like a magician by making crazy things happen out of thin air at the enthrallment of his audience. This kind of representation of God seems to only confirm stereotypes that agnostics and atheists have of believers and their "superstitious" beliefs in an almighty God, i.e., this reminds me of old ladies who come upon potato chips or croutons bearing the likeness of Jesus.

Yet, I now have a greater context for interpreting this event. That context is a lifetime of prayer, with its day-by-day outcomes and observations. Is it superstitious to say that God would manifest his glory to a youth, when for a lifetime this same God has answered prayers *daily*, even for what some might call trivial requests (such as an answer to an urgent telephone call or a prayer for a parking spot)? It might be faithless ingratitude to ignore it when God answers an honest request of the heart.

Consider the humorous example of the man who was in a lather to find a parking spot for a very important business meeting. The man cried out to God and lifted his head to heaven: "God, if you find me a parking spot, I will go to church every Sunday for the rest of my life and give up swearing." Suddenly, a spot miraculously opened up right before him by the front door. "Never mind, I found one," he said.

Is it trivial to think God does this, or is it ingratitude to believe that God *doesn't*? One can only know a miracle, even when it may appear to be trivial, in the context of a lifetime of answered prayer. Likewise, we can only adequately answer the question of whether this was merely a coincidence or a certain *God*-incident from a fuller knowledge of who God is and what God does, questions which I hope to explore in the next section, "God in History."

In Exodus 20, the Bible tells the story of Moses with the Israelites during the exodus from Egypt. At Mount Sinai, God spoke in the presence of all the people assembled at the foot of the mountain. Smoke and fire arose from the mountain as he spoke in the hearing of all the Israelites. The people were terrified and asked Moses to go up on the mountain by himself to speak with God so the people would not have the terror of listening to almighty God speak. The Israelites were afraid God's voice would kill them!

Trivial though it may sound, my experience on that night under the stars had a similar effect. That same reverential dread came upon me when I saw the second shooting star and felt overwhelmed by God's powerful presence.

What I had learned several years earlier, that truly a First Cause, a Creator of the universe, existed, was now brought to bear on me personally. Now the First Cause was responding to human conversation and entering an interactive relationship with me. I learned almost nothing more about God that night except that Something was alive up there with a responsive mind, and whatever it was, it seemed to be able to give a direct response to my personal words of request.

MORE THAN A FIRST CAUSE

This discovery didn't instantly make me a Christian. I was still basically agnostic about many traditional beliefs, and I didn't know anything about Jesus Christ or the Bible. Yet, this was an immense breakthrough that some contemporary thinkers in religion fail to make. Some scholars writing on faith matters would agree that there is a power or mind that transcends the natural world, maybe in terms similar to what I expressed in my discovery of the First Cause. Even the foremost atheist in Great Britain in the twentieth century, Antony Flew, has just recently admitted that there has to be a Creator God somewhere.[21] But for many scholars, God never interferes with the natural world and does not actually hear or answer prayer—God is not personally interactive. The name for this in religion is *deism*.

That night under the open heavens, I made a breakthrough that I have proven over and over again: whatever it is transcending the natural world responds to our words and our hearts. This Power possesses mind and intellect.

The discovery of the mind of God didn't just happen in isolation to a boy several decades ago. God's mind, revealed in the intelligent design of the universe that we observe in nature, intrigues many scientists in the twenty-first century who long to explore the evidence for God from the architecture of the universe he has made.

A SCIENTIFIC DEBATE

There is a growing and powerful debate among scientists today over whether the theory of evolution can truly explain the occurrence of all life forms due to the laws of nature acting on events by sheer randomness and blind chance, or whether life can better be understood as created by intelligent design by an Intelligent Designer.

Some scientists are still convinced that the greatest thought humanity has ever had is the idea of evolution, as expressed in Charles Darwin's seminal work *On the Origin of Species*, written nearly one hundred and fifty years ago! Because of Darwin, many biologists today accept most of the teachings of evolution. As Francis Collins, the director of the National Human Genome Research Institute, has observed: "Nearly all working biologists accept that the principles of variation and natural selection explain how multiple species evolved from a common ancestor over very long periods of time." [22]

But what for many years has been a common acceptance of evolution is weakening. Growing numbers of legitimate scientists are questioning many of the basic ideas of Darwinian evolution and are rethinking the whole evolutionary concept of life coming by random chance and the laws of nature from a common ancestor over millions of years.

This fierce debate is chronicled in very informative books (like *By Design or by Chance* by Canadian science author Denyse O'Leary) and in newspaper and magazine feature stories such as the recent "Evolution Wars" cover story in *Time* magazine. This growing debate is creating great uneasiness among traditional schools of evolutionists about even entering any debate on evolution.

As *Time* observes:

Many scientists have been reluctant to engage in a debate with advocates of intelligent design because to do so would legitimize the claim that there's meaningful debate about evolution. "I'm concerned about implying that there is some sort of scientific argument going on. There's not," says noted British biologist Richard Dawkins, professor of the public understanding of science at Oxford University.[23]

The growing doubts about evolution don't come from religious thinkers or philosophers, but from the science of the origin of life itself. One of the major scientists supporting intelligent design is Michael Behe, biochemistry professor at Lehigh University and senior fellow of the Discovery Institute. *Time* reports his position:

> I'm still not against evolution on theological grounds. I'm against it on scientific grounds. I think God could have made life using apparently random mutation and natural selection. But my reading of the scientific evidence is that he did not do it that way, that there was a more active guiding. I think that we are all descended from some single cell in the distant past and later parts of life were intentionally produced as a result of intelligent activity. As a Christian, I say that intelligence is very likely to be God.[24]

The science of evolution is also changing—possibly significantly—due to the massive shift in the science behind the origin of the universe, that is, in the field of astronomy. Major discoveries in the science of astronomy have raised a loud voice in the debate over intelligent design. What has happened in the science of the stars?

THE "BIG BANG" THAT BEGAN THE UNIVERSE

To understand recent changes, it is first necessary to see what was believed about the origin of the universe at the time when Darwin wrote *On the Origin of Species*. In the 1850s, astronomers and other scientists generally thought that the universe was eternal, without a beginning or an end. It just existed forever, with random change operating under the laws of nature. However, astronomy changed in the early twentieth century. As science author Denyse O'Leary writes:

> Then, in 1927, an obscure Belgian priest and cosmologist, George Lemaitre, proposed that the universe popped into existence between 10 and 20 billion years ago, beginning with a single point.[25]

This radical idea overturned the entire field of cosmology, that part of astronomy that seeks to understand the origin of the universe. Lemaitre was theorizing a beginning in time for everything that exists in the universe, a truly revolutionary idea that had huge consequences in other fields of knowledge, especially in Darwin's field of evolution.

Learning from the Stars

Briefly, here is the history of this revolution. It was American astronomer Edwin Hubble (1889–1953) who discovered in 1929 that the galaxies were moving away from each other, the most distant ones at the greatest speed. Now, any theory about the beginning of the universe had to explain why, *if the universe is eternal*, the galaxies we now see on a starry night have not entirely moved away from us. The evidence suggested that everything had begun from a massive explosion.

British astronomer Sir Frederick Hoyle (1916–2001) tried vigorously to disprove this theory of a finite universe, beginning in time and space, with what he termed in one of his papers as the "big bang." His antagonism stemmed from the fact that this theory so strongly implied the idea of a Creator creating everything out of nothing at a finite time in measurable space.

Hoyle and several of his colleagues were determined to explain this expanding universe through the "steady state theory," wherein the universe was expanding not because of an original big bang but because of a steady creation of new matter out of nothing, a theory which returned Hoyle to an eternal universe. As an atheist, Hoyle hated the theory of a finite universe in time and space because, as O'Leary comments, "he recognized its theological implications and he didn't like them at all."[26] Hoyle's theory was never accepted by most astronomers because he never found evidence for the creation of new matter. While Hoyle never did find a satisfactory answer to the big bang, he still did do valuable research along the way.

Other discoveries cemented the big bang theory during Hoyle's lifetime. A major—and unexpected—advance came in 1965 from two physicists, Arno Penzias and Robert Wilson, who accidentally discovered the cosmic radiation that is assumed to be left over from the big bang. It spreads out as space expands in all directions, at a temperature just a little below three degrees above absolute zero. O'Leary writes:

> In 1990, NASA's Cosmic Background Explorer (COBE) satellite made more accurate measurements. The atmosphere was tense as scientists gathered at the Goddard Space Flight Center near Washington, D.C. to hear the numbers read out. The numbers vindicated the Big Bang beautifully, which caused the head of the team, George Smoot, to say: "I felt I was looking God in the face."[27]

What are the implications to evolution if the universe had a beginning in time and space? Darwin, and many like him, didn't know what we know now. In their "eternal universe," it wasn't hard to believe that there had been all the time you would ever need for every life form we know today to come into existence by sheer chance, influenced only by the laws of nature. But things are different now.

THE COSMIC LOTTERY

Denyse O'Leary suggests the very helpful illustration of a lottery to explain the implications of an eternal universe.[28] A lottery ticket offers a chance to win the prize solely by the random laws of nature—but that random win is only possible by a completely honest process, blind chance working under the laws of nature. If this is not an honest draw but is rigged by a cheater, someone will consistently win far beyond what random chance would suggest is possible.

If you buy a lottery ticket in an eternal universe, then your number will win an infinite number of times because there is an unending amount of time for you to keep winning over and over again. In this case, there is nothing suspicious about winning over and over again, because you have enough time for this to keep happening. Nothing is rigged; there is no reason to suspect a dishonest agent for your unending winning ticket, because you have an unending amount of time in which to win.

In the lottery for the evolution of life, every form of new life that emerges and survives would count as a clear win. If a cheater has rigged the results, then an entirely unexpected series of successful life forms would emerge even when mere random chance would result in much less or nothing happening. Great suspicion arises that someone has been interfering and messing around with the outcome when there are so many consistent major wins, far beyond what random chance in nature would allow.

This eternal lottery ticket is at the heart of Darwinian evolution. Look at what could happen if the universe was eternal: an eternal universe gives great credibility to the idea that every possible life form could have time to come into existence and evolve into something else. This represents a win with our lottery ticket. Insofar as living things win the right to exist and mutate into something else, our lottery tickets keep winning again and again and again, until you reach our present day with the winning design that the universe displays!

Moreover, given an eternal amount of time for all this happen, there is no hint of Someone rigging the lottery. There is no dishonest agent or designer interfering with a natural process working by random chance operating under natural laws because it happens over an eternal amount of time. Thus, although there is the undeniable *appearance* of design in the universe, there is little credibility in the idea of a Designer (God). The intelligent design we see could reasonably result from pure natural selection given an eternal amount of time.

Now, look at how this entire scientific scenario changes with a finite universe beginning and ending in finite time and measurable space. According to most astronomers today, the universe is only about ten to fourteen billion years old.[29] That's about two years of evolution for every living person present in the world today. If for this limited time you could issue lottery tickets, look at how many times—not over an eternity, but within a very limited period of finite time—your ticket would win. Again, and again, and again, as life took form from that first living cell, through complex algae, then grass and flowers, then fish, and birds, and animals, and humankind—you win over and over and over again! To believe that all this comes only randomly by chance working through the blind laws of nature is staggering.

What incredible luck we have! You might well be suspicious that this whole lottery is rigged by a hidden agent. How else could we be winning so many times in a row in such a brief history of chance happenings? Someone is interfering with the results! (This "dishonest agent," rigging our ticket to win more and more in the intelligent design we observe, is completely consistent with the portrait of the biblical Creator God we will come to know in the next chapter. The Cheater interfering with random chance by bringing to the world all these intricate, detailed, surviving new life forms is God.)

Enter a growing number of scientists, according to *Time* magazine,[30] who are questioning the suspicious succession of wins in this "chance" lottery for life on earth. Hence the building debate among scientists trying to explain why it looks as if this lottery has been rigged by a hidden agent, giving us the history of remarkable wins in all our complex design and purpose.

CREATING A SINGLE CELL—LIFE'S SMALLEST FORM

A major contribution to the present debate comes from biochemist Michael Behe in his book, *Darwin's Black Box*.[31] Darwin tried to explain all life forms in terms of nature's laws and random chance only, but Behe and other scientists are observing a third factor in the formation of all living things—that of design. Design is not merely a matter of faith: it can be observed in organisms and scientifically studied.

Behe gives a brilliant example of design in the simplest form of all living things, a single living cell. His point is that a living cell is "irreducibly complex." O'Leary clarifies this for us:

> He means there are no "simple" cell systems that could just arise by chance from the six organic elements (calcium, carbon, hydrogen, nitrogen, oxygen, and phosphorus) and then evolve into complex cell systems. That is because there is no simple way of doing the jobs that these systems do. A creature with a simpler arrangement could not live at all. A little malfunction here or there, and the cell does not evolve to a higher form of life; it dies. One reason that cells are complex is that they must use molecular machinery to force elements and chemicals to do things that they do not normally do.[32]

Irreducible complexity means that a system could not function if any of its parts were missing or defective. Without the agency of design, no irreducibly complex system arises. Darwin's natural selection cannot choose a system that does not yet exist! The internal design of the cell can be studied for its complexity and design, but it cannot be reduced to a simpler form of life that evolved into this first living cell.

The first living cell is the first win for our lottery ticket, and it looks like it is not just the outcome of the laws of probability and chance.

LIFE HAS NEVER BEEN CREATED BY SCIENTISTS

The debate becomes much more intense when we see the results from two scientists who tried to create a living cell in a test tube. In 1953, Stanley Miller and Harold Urey mixed together the gases which they thought were present in the earth's early atmosphere (methane, ammonia, hydrogen, and water), shot electricity the size of lightning bolts through it, and created amino acids, which are the necessary building blocks of life. Their experiment was duplicated with a huge flurry of worldwide publicity declaring that life had finally been created in a test tube. (The publicity was somewhat misleading—amino acids are fundamental for life to exist, but they are not life in themselves. Really, what occurred was something like making tar.)

Despite this popular claim, the feat of creating a single living cell has never been achieved by any scientist anywhere in the world despite unending efforts in our own day. None of the origin-of-life researchers have ever been able to successfully create life!

Where, then, did the first living cell come from, that living organism which is irreducibly complex, if it cannot be accounted for in terms of random chance blindly struggling around under the laws of nature? It has been impossible to create this simplest form of life from any mixture of chemistry and energy in the best experiments in the laboratories of the world—so how did it arise in the beginning?

What the Common Person Believes

While the debate rages among scientists, there are many North Americans who may not know the science of the origin of life, but they do firmly believe that God designed and created it. In a Harris poll conducted in 2005, 54 percent of Americans said they did not believe humans had developed from an earlier species—up from 45 percent who held that view in 1994.[33]

Why such a pronounced disconnection between the "science" of evolution and the disbelief of the general population? Is it, as some atheists claim, that the general public is uninformed of science, in need of a "heavenly Father" in a threatening world, or just plain stupid? Let me give some unscientific illustrations from everyday life to help the unbelieving evolutionist see how the general population thinks. Many people have a very limited scientific knowledge of evolution, but there are some things most people clearly perceive.

Often, in the warmer weather of the spring, summer, and fall, I read my Bible and pray on the front porch of our log home on the shores of Lake Erie. I see a hummingbird sipping nectar from the Rose of Sharon blossoms or the orange lilies in the front lawn and gardens. This scene of impressive beauty speaks to me of the great design and purpose in living things, aiding me in the lifting of my prayers to the Intelligent Designer behind these perceptions. I can almost see the fingerprints of the Creator in the tiny wings of the hummingbird or on the petals of the lilies. Here we find the common adage in action: "Seeing is believing!"

Many, if not almost all, people around the world experience the design and beauty of the Creator's intelligent design. The lyrics of popular recording artist Sarah McLachlan's song "Ordinary Miracle" speak of the natural world reflecting something truly wonderful—miracles from God, which imply an Intelligent Designer. McLachlan sings of it not being unusual for everything to look so beautiful, for the order of the seasons to play out, for snow to fall and seeds to grow—all evidence of the astonishing ordinary miracles we see every day! The song sees God's amazing touch in the rain falling on the earth and the birds knowing when to fly south in the winter and return in the spring, and in the myriads of God's blessings today and every day.

Such experiences of life are common to many people. It is not that believers in these ordinary miracles are stupid or don't know science. It's just overwhelmingly evident that this world is intelligently designed and really experienced as "ordinary miracles" from God!

It may be that science (or scientists, in some cases) has not caught up with the appearance of intelligent design which the general public sees over and over again—in the chasm of the Grand

Canyon, a French seascape on the English Channel, the emotional harmony of a symphony orchestra, or many other experiences. We are surrounded not only by the appearance of intelligent design, but the convincing perception of a Creator-Designer.

Sometimes, to see intelligent design is just a proper way of looking at something. Michael Behe, a practicing Catholic, believes the hand of the designer is self-evident. "That's why most people disbelieve Darwinian evolution. People go out and look at the trees and say, 'Nay.'"[34]

Fearfully and Wonderfully Made

Sometimes we live in such a secular culture of doubt that we cannot see the true nature of things. One of the greatest inspirational books for me as a young minister was the book *Fearfully and Wonderfully Made*, written by Philip Yancey and world-renowned hand surgeon and rehabilitation specialist Dr. Paul Brand, who for eighteen years did brilliant pioneering work on the disease of leprosy in India.

In the book, Dr. Brand relates how the human body is beautifully made, with insights he gained from the treatment of lepers in India. At one point, Dr. Brand was on a demanding series of speaking engagements in the United States and fell quite sick on his way home to London. When he got to his hotel room, he took his sock off to discover to his absolute horror that his left heel had no feeling. He pricked his foot several times with a needle, with blood coming out but no pain. "A dreaded fear worse than nausea gripped my stomach," he writes. "After seven years of working with leprosy patients, had it finally happened? Was I now to be a patient myself?"[35]

The next morning, after a night's rest, he pricked his foot again and with indescribable joy, yelled from pain! From that experience, he writes of the marvelous nature of human skin:

> Think of the variety of stimuli your skin monitors each day: wind, particles, parasites, changes in pressure,

temperature, humidity, light, radiation. Skin is tough enough to withstand the rigorous pounding of jogging on asphalt, yet sensitive enough to have bare toes tickled by a light breeze. The word *touch* swells with such a plethora of meanings and images that in many dictionaries including the *Oxford English*, its definition runs the longest of any entry. I can hardly think of a human activity—sports, music, art, cooking, mechanics, sex—that does not vitally rely on touch. (Perhaps pure mathematics?)

Touch is the most alert of our senses when we sleep, and it is the one that seems to invigorate us emotionally: consider the lovers' embrace, the contented sigh after a massage, the cuddling of a baby, the sting of a hot shower.[36]

As Dr. Brand observes, something as basic as the healthy sense of touch reveals a divine hand at work. Does the world exhibit intelligent design, pointing to a Designer who possesses power, intellect, and will? It is far, far more believable that our world is intelligently designed by God and that our bodies are "fearfully and wonderfully made"—as in the book title by Yancey and Brand, taken from Psalm 139:14—than that this amazing world has happened by random chance working under the sightless laws of nature. I just cannot believe such a blind and sterile theory.

O'Leary quotes astronomer Robert Jastrow, writing in his book *God and the Astronomers*:

For the scientist who has lived by his faith in the power of reason, the story ends like a bad dream. He has scaled the mountains of ignorance, he is about to conquer the highest peak; as he pulls himself over the final rock, he is greeted by a bank of theologians who have been sitting there for centuries.[37]

In summary, if our argument for God as the First Cause demonstrates God's immense and unimaginable power, and we then add from intelligent design the intellect and omnipotent mind of God, we must conclude that God is capable of any action in our physical world and possesses a mind able to form a personal relationship with the human mind and personality. This is a God big enough to believe in as we open our Bibles!

It must be stressed in this chapter that if God is all-powerful as the First Cause of the cosmos, and if God has an unsearchable mind as the Intelligent Designer, then God's acts of power in our world are not only completely possible, but even likely. This forms our major assumptions in our search for God: the First Cause has power, and the Intelligent Designer has mind. This Being appears capable of interacting with human beings, who also have intelligent minds capable of responding to a God like this. This powerful, intelligent Being is what we are now looking for!

Do we have here yet the Christian concept of a loving God who faithfully hears and answers the prayers of the believer's longing heart? We see the possibility for all this, as I concluded under the night sky, but we need much more *self-disclosure* from God to confirm that it is God's hand and not blind, random coincidence that works on a daily basis in human life. Where, apart from nature, can we find out more about God?

Hopefully, the reader will see that the most reasonable step that any intelligent and sensitive person can now take is to seek more about God in the history of the human race, looking for any further evidence for knowing this divine Being.

THE COMING SEISMIC SHIFT

After the second shooting star on that starry night in Maple, some things were changing for me. I graduated and entered high school, and at the same time met the Reverend Jack Cooper, who moved into our town and began a young people's Bible study group in our local church. I was about to discover that the powerful, intelligent, and personally responsive God who had responded to my words that night under the stars was the same God who unveiled his glory in the history related by the Christian Bible.

The Bible became the starting point for all the exciting questions about God bursting in my mind and heart during my high school years. The days of my discovery of God in the Bible were beginning!

PART 2

God in History

CHAPTER 3
The Book with a Storyline

N ow that we have started by experiencing God in nature, we ask: "Is there any record of this God interacting in world history? Has God done so, and if so, when, where, and how?"

What more obvious place for us to start to look for answers than in the religions of the world?

Like the scientist pulling himself up to the bank of theologians, we find that most information available about God or gods is found in the history, philosophy, and teachings of the different religions of the world. Despite the wrongs world religions may have done, their apparent irrationality at times, and the fanaticism they sometimes exhibit, the study of God in different cultures and religions is unavoidable if we are to gain any additional knowledge of God beyond natural theology and our own personal experience.

It is not, however, necessary to painstakingly study every religion in the world. One shortcut is to read a reliable summary of world cultures, religions, and cults. One highly recommended volume, by Christian scholar and evangelical apologist Professor James Beverley, is the new compendium of world religions called *Nelson's Illustrated Guide to Religions*.[38]

For our purposes, we'll look at the journey of two intellectual young men who *didn't* take any shortcuts in studying world cultures and religions in their search for God. For the sake of convenience, we'll let them represent our common pursuit for truth in world cultures and religions.

Please travel with me to two different parts of the world: first to Malaysia and then to Cairo, Egypt, where two young men of great intellectual ability try to answer the questions about God by reading all the holy books of world religions. Both these men were interviewed as guests on my national Canadian telecast, *Reachout for Life*, where they gave their life stories.

T.V. THOMAS'S QUEST FOR GOD

Dr. T.V. Thomas grew up in Muslim-dominated Malaysia and fervently sought for God by reading "two hundred books on philosophy, psychology, and religion, including all their major holy books," he told me. He was desperate to find answers in his quest for God. T.V.'s appetite for more and more truth grew as he read books like the Koran, the Buddhist and Hindu Scriptures, philosophy, psychology, and the biographies of religious leaders. He then read the Jewish and Christian Bible and was immediately struck by how different the Bible was from all the other holy books.

"The great religious books had very high teaching on ethics and how to live a good, moral life," he said. "As I started to read the Bible, I saw it has a beginning with the creation of the universe out of nothing. Then it describes the origin of all living things. Then there was the beginning of human history with our first parents, Adam and Eve.

"The Bible has a storyline unlike any of the other books!" T.V. stated. "It is rooted in the history of Abraham and the people of Israel through the times and historical places of the prophets, priests, and kings of the Old Testament.

"The New Testament is just as rooted in history, with the continuing storyline of the life and teachings of Jesus, the history of the early church in the Acts of the Apostles, and ending with the last judgment of humanity and eternity in heaven recorded in the last book of the Bible in Revelation."

The Bible was so different that he began to read it through a second time. And when he came to Jesus's promise in John 10:10, "I have come that they may have life, and have it to the full" (NIV), he paused and solemnly asked God for that gift of life. Nothing changed immediately—until he woke up the next morning and felt that he was an entirely new man! He has never turned back from God's promise, given to him in the Bible that night, and has had a remarkable international career for Jesus Christ.

Later in life he went to seminary, received a PhD from Fuller University in California, taught as a professor at a college in Alberta, and served as chairman of the board of directors for the Christian and Missionary Alliance Church in Canada.

T.V. Thomas began as a young man by going to the religions of the world and reading current philosophy and psychology, and he found a book that totally turned him around by its unexpected storyline. That book, the Christian Bible, was the instrument through which God came into his life in a powerful, living, personal relationship—as so much more than simply a God seen in nature.

CLEARING SALT FLATS IN THE EGYPTIAN DESERT

The other young man, Tawfik George, grew up in Egypt. Extremely pessimistic about life, he thought occasionally of killing himself. He fervently wanted to know if there was a God, and he too began to read all the holy Scriptures of Islam, Hinduism, Buddhism, Baha'i, and Sikhism. Buddhist meditation leading to enlightenment especially attracted him.

Then Tawfik George began to read the Bible. "The Bible is a different book from all the others," Tawfik explained. "It seems to have a place in history, both with the people and the geography that I am already familiar with."

At that time, being a physical education teacher, he already knew the value of meditation. But when he read the beginning of the Gospel of John, "In the beginning was the Word; and the Word was with God and the Word was God," he went beyond meditating on the book and prayed to this God. A few verses further on, in verse 14, Tawfik read, "And the Word took on human flesh and dwelt among us and we have seen His glory, the glory of the one and only Son of the Father." Tawfik was in awe of this assertion of God coming into our world, seen and attested to by the writer of this gospel.

Although Tawfik had never had anyone explain to him the meaning of the Christian faith or how to become a Christian, when he read the first fourteen verses in John's gospel he believed them to be the truth: God existed and had entered our world in Jesus Christ.

Though he says that he tries to read a new book almost every night of his life, Tawfik said, "I read the Bible completely through two or three more times and now I believed and found an immense purpose for living."

Tawfik was immediately a different man, with an immense purpose for living, and he longed to do something to help the many unemployed men in Egypt. Soon he cleared a salt flat in the desert and began to build the Think and Do Center in the desert north of Cairo, where thousands of men have come for practical vocational and spiritual training lasting between six weeks and six months. They learn carpentry, plumbing, cooking, barbering, computers, and pastoral training for lay ministries in churches in Egypt. The Think and Do Center has a multimillion-dollar budget each year that Tawfik raises by sheer prayer and faith alone! Tawfik is a living saint in this isolated part of the Middle East.

Just as T.V. Thomas did, Tawfik George searched the religions and philosophies of the world's cultures seeking for God. They both remarked how different it was to discover the Bible. This book was so utterly different and unique that they couldn't put it down until they found God in its words!

ST. AUGUSTINE: "PICK IT UP AND READ!"

Historically, the Bible has had an immense power in bringing faith to people seeking for God. St. Augustine, in the fourth century, resisted Christianity and lived a completely dissolute and immoral life as a young man. His mother, Monica, prayed fervently for him. Then, after meeting a Christian mentor in St. Ambrose of Milano, he one day "heard" God speak to him: "Pick it up and read, pick it up and read."[39] St. Augustine picked up the Bible on the table in front of him, and that book so impacted his life that he accepted Christ and became one of Christianity's greatest thinkers and saints.

In learning from these men, let us examine the Bible as a unique reference point and resource in our search for knowledge of God. Why the Bible? Here follows the main reason why we can and should turn to the Bible for knowledge of God beyond what we know from the natural world alone.

AN ATHEIST AND JESUS TELL TWO PARABLES

What value does the Bible have, if any at all, in our search for the God whom we feel might be there? Obviously, the Bible is a significant part of the culture of world religions. However, is the Bible only useful for personal devotions and personal faith, or does it possess objective, sound, concrete evidence for our discussion of God? Does anything truly set it apart from the other holy books in the world religious scene?

Listen to one of the most popular and widely read atheists, Richard Dawkins, writing on the Bible in *The God Delusion*:

> Although Jesus probably existed, reputable biblical scholars do not in general regard the New Testament (and obviously the Old Testament) as a reliable record of what actually happened in history, and I shall not consider the bible as evidence for any kind of deity.[40]

Dawkins's sweeping statement demonstrates little more than his biblical illiteracy. The Bible has been ripped apart and "discredited" by some authorities (Dawkins isn't one of them), but as we will see, the Bible is "necessary, sufficient, and reliable," as worded in the Presbyterian Church in Canada's *Living Faith*,[41] for all of our knowledge of God! It is in fact historical, and it is in fact reliable. This chapter will attempt to prove the complete reliability of the Christian Scriptures for our knowledge of God.

Two parables demonstrate how much the Bible brings to our discussion of God beyond all that we know from nature: one from a former atheist, Antony Flew, and the second from Jesus of Nazareth.

Writing in *The Philosophy of Religion*,[42] Antony Flew tells the parable of the invisible gardener. Two explorers travel through a jungle and fall upon a clearing of flowers and many weeds. The first explorer says, "There must be a gardener who tends this plot." The other disagrees.

The explorers set up a tent and watch for the gardener, but none is seen. "Perhaps the gardener is invisible," the one says. So they put up a fence with electric wire and patrol with bloodhounds. However, the wire never moves, the electric fence is never discharged, and the hounds never cry out because of an intruder.

In Flew's own words:

Yet the believer is still not convinced. "But there is a gardener, invisible, intangible, insensible to electric shocks, a gardener who has no scent and makes no sound, a gardener who comes secretly to look after the garden which he loves." At last the Sceptic despairs, "But what remains of your original assertion? Just how does what you call an invisible, intangible, eternally elusive gardener differ from an imaginary gardener or even from no gardener at all?"[43]

Flew's point is that if you keep changing and qualifying what you mean by "God" in describing his relationship to the natural world, you do not end up with any meaningful description of God at all. In Flew's most memorable sentence, he concludes: "A fine brash hypothesis may thus be killed by inches, the death by a thousand qualifications."[44]

If all we had to go on in our search for God was our personal experience of this "garden" of our natural world, then could we ever know anything much at all about the Gardener except his power as the Creator and his mind as the Designer?

Now, listen to a parable told by Jesus Christ. Jesus told many parables in his public ministry, based upon well-known and commonly observed occupations and events of his day. Jesus told this very significant parable in Jerusalem during the last week of his life.

Like that of Antony Flew, this story is about a garden, but instead of a garden of flowers and weeds in a jungle, this is a vineyard with tenants who live in the garden and tend it, renting it from a landowner who planted it and went away for a long time.

The story Jesus is telling here has a very real historical background. Jesus is speaking here about the "garden" of the promised land of Israel, which God gave as a vineyard to the Jews to enjoy. This is not an imaginary garden in the jungle, but an allegorical story about the real history of the tenants in God's vineyard of Israel.

At harvest time the Land Owner sent a servant to the tenant so they would give him some of the fruit of the vineyard. But the tenants beat him and sent him away empty-handed. He sent another servant, but that one also they beat and treated shamefully and sent away empty-handed. He sent still a third, and they wounded him and threw him out.

Then the owner of the vineyard said, "What shall I do? I will send my son, whom I love, perhaps they will respect him." But when the tenants saw him, they talked the matter over. "This is the heir," they said. "Let's kill him and the inheritance will be ours." So they threw him out of the vineyard and killed him.

What then will the owner of the vineyard do to them?
He will come and kill those tenants and give the vineyard
to others. (Luke 20:10–16, NIV)

Jesus alludes here to the prophets, who were the servants of the
"Land Owner," God. The prophets were often persecuted by the Israelites. We have their words in their books in the Old Testament.
And the owner's son is Jesus himself, the Son of God, who finally
came to fulfill Israel's calling and promises.

Luke concludes the story with this narrative: "The teachers of
the law and the chief priests looked for a way to arrest him immediately, because they knew he had spoken this parable against them.
But they were afraid of the people" (Luke 20:19, NIV).

THE BIBLE BRINGS HISTORY INTO OUR KNOWLEDGE OF GOD FROM NATURE

While Antony Flew only has the garden of the natural world,
Jesus's parable tells of a garden *in the actual history and geography of
Israel* as recorded in the Bible.

The Bible contains so much more than what is found in the best
of all of our personal experiences of nature! Because they are cen-
tered on specific times and places in the real world, the Old and New
Testaments offer a huge treasure of information to help us discover
far more than could ever be available to two explorers debating the
merits of the natural world's garden!

THE STYLE OF WRITING HISTORY

But is the Bible a reliable source of information—or is it shot
through and through with unreliable and confusing mythology and
contradictions? Is it, as Dawkins says, lacking in "evidence for any
kind of deity"?[45]

Writing in *The God Delusion*, Dawkins comments further on the
Christian Bible:

"Do these people never open the book they believe is the literal truth? Why don't they notice those glaring contradictions?"[46]

Dawkins records what he thinks are massive contradictions in the narrative in Matthew and Luke on the genealogy and birth of Jesus Christ. He says that Matthew traces Joseph's descent from King David through twenty-eight independent generations, while Luke has forty-one generations. Worse, he says, there is almost no overlap in the names on the two lists of genealogy.[47]

What Professor Dawkins needs most here is to sit down with an intelligent group of Christians in a Bible study to address these problems! If he did, he might learn that Matthew chose to trace the genealogy of Jesus through his stepfather Joseph, since Matthew stresses the Jewishness of Jesus. Luke emphasizes the role of women in his gospel and most likely traced the genealogy of Jesus through his mother, Mary, accounting for the different names and numbers of family members. Also, as was common practice in the genealogies of the ancient Jews, some of the families in the genealogies would go by different first or last names, accounting for additional differences.

The apparent contradictions pointed out by critics of the Bible can only be resolved through careful study of the text. It should also be expected that there will be different accounts of the same incident because that is the basic model for reporting history. For example, I occasionally watch four news networks at night: BBC World News, CNN Situation Room, Global National News, and CTV Evening News, the last two produced in Canada. They cover many of the same events but from different camera shots, interviewing different witnesses, and possibly standing upon different editorial viewpoints. What do we have here? A terrible mess of contradictions? Not at all! It is the nature of history to have different accounts of the same events. The Bible is no different, and many "contradictions" can be explained this way.

Take, for example, the apparent contradiction in the story of Jesus cleansing the temple of the money changers, recorded in all four of the histories of Jesus's life in Matthew 21:12–13, Mark 11:15–17, Luke 19:45–46, and John 2:12–16. The first three gospels contain much of the same order and details of Jesus's ministry, and they place the cleansing of the temple in Jerusalem during the last week of his life. John's gospel changes this order of events and places it at the very beginning of Jesus's ministry in chapter 2. Is this what Dawkins would call a "glaring contradiction"?

It might appear so, unless we understand the role of the reporter in editing his work in the order that best suits the telling of the story. That is just a fact of reporting history: an editor can arrange material in his own way. The details are the same in all four Gospels, but John puts the story first in Jesus's ministry (although not indicating that it actually occurred in this particular sequence of time). He might have placed it first for his particular editorial emphasis on the future ministry Jesus was to have. For John, the cleansing of the temple prefigures the coming conflict between Jesus and the authorities in Jerusalem, and placing it early foreshadows the coming battle.

Many students of the Bible and apologists for the faith, like Britain's C.S. Lewis, Canada's Joe Boot, and America's Ravi Zacharias, can satisfyingly explain every so-called contradiction in the Bible in reasonable and responsible ways.

DO WE KNOW THE ORIGINAL WORDS IN THE BIBLE?

Someone may ask, "Do we know the original, accurate words of the Bible?" Some critics point out that we no longer possess the very first, original books of the Bible by the named authors. This creates a great problem for some inquirers: we have none of the extant copies of the original books in the Bible, and some of these books may have been written several decades after the events they record. Then does anyone know the true Bible?

A New Testament professor, Dr. Tim Geddert, at Fresno Pacific Biblical Seminary in Fresno, California, said at a conference in Port

Rowan, Ontario in 2006 that "Many people believe that no one knows what the real Bible says—except for one group of people," he explained. "They are the professors who teach the Old and New Testament. And these scholars know almost exactly every word in the original text!"

Another problem exists in the minds of some: because most Christians are only reading translations of the Bible into other languages, it's argued that we are not really reading the real Word of God. This problem can be clearly resolved by understanding what I call the "target view" of Scripture. Many people have had the experience of shooting an arrow or a bullet at a target. On the target, there are wider and wider circles for recording the accuracy of the shot. Everyone taking a shot aims at the dead center, but you can still score even if your shot lands outside the bull's-eye by hitting one of the outer circles.

Synonyms, or similar words used in different translations, can all hit the target with varying degrees of accuracy, all having a valid meaning! But differences aside, they *do* hit the target somewhere. Even within Scripture, quotes from the Old Testament in the New Testament text may have a different order of thoughts expressed, or different words used than in the original text. But the quoted Scripture has identical meaning with the original passage. It scores on the target.

THE GOSPEL ACCORDING TO LARRY

On my television program, *Reachout for Life*, I often quote the Bible from memory. My producer, Mr. Michael Hanley, calls this "the gospel according to Larry." But my quotations are always very close to most translations. People will not fail to hear the Word of God even as I loosely quote it!

Canada is home to many people whose first language is not English. Yet, when listening carefully, it is almost always possible to understand the conversation with someone who is newly learning English. Their speech falls within the target. Likewise, approximation counts in translating the original words of the Bible.

In fact, all the Christian translations of the Bible, from the most accurate RSV and American Standard to the very literary versions translated for popular reading, like *The Living Bible* or *The Message*, hit the target in such a compelling way that they often bring new insights into God's original Word with greater understanding!

Reader beware, however: there are translations of the Bible from groups who do not consider themselves Christian, and their texts can be seen to include flagrant errors leading to different beliefs altogether. Their translations of the Bible, in significant places, do not land on the target at all.

University of Manchester New Testament scholar F.F. Bruce, writing in his book *The English Bible*,[48] said that not one doctrine of the Christian faith is in jeopardy because of the differences in translation or variant readings in all the Christian translations of the English Bible. In other words, all the translations hit the target, even though some are further from the bull's-eye than others.

AIM FOR THE CENTER

But what about that bull's-eye? That is what every pastor and student of the Bible tries to find when reading or translating the original words in the Scriptures. In fact, every word written in the original Hebrew or Greek by the prophets and apostles in Scripture *did* hit the exact center of God's inspired Word in their original documents. And this brings us back to the question of whether we actually know the original words from the first text God inspired the biblical authors to write, or whether they have been lost or changed over the centuries.

To answer this, consider the exhibit of the Dead Sea Scrolls that tours the museums of the world: scrolls of the Bible found by Bedouin shepherds in the mid-twentieth century. Specifically, consider the book of the prophet Isaiah, who lived c. 740–681 BC, found there at Qumran on the shore of the Dead Sea. This particular scroll had been copied in its entirety before or around the time of the birth of Christ. The original book of Isaiah, which we no longer possess, was written in Hebrew and has been copied over and over again throughout the Maccabaean, Roman, medieval, Reformation, Enlightenment, and modern times over these last twenty-five-hundred years, all the way down to our own time. So here is the miracle: the present Hebrew text of Isaiah that we have today is almost identical in every word to the ancient Dead Sea Scroll of Isaiah found at Qumran!

Because of this, we can expect that the other books in the Bible, including all those of the New Testament period written at about the same time as this text of Isaiah from the Dead Sea Scrolls was copied, would be copied as accurately as the ancient text of Isaiah. Thus it appears that we have a reliable knowledge of the text of the original Bible!

The writers of the books of the Bible lived over a two thousand-year period, possessing different personalities, mental abilities, and literary talents. The Bible possesses a special status all of its own. Scholars and church leaders must have the utmost respect and reverence for the authority and integrity of the Holy Scriptures, both in terms of how its content gives it the character of being God's Word and in terms of the authority it possesses to tell the story of true history.

The Bible speaks about its own authority in 2 Timothy 3:16, claiming that it is accurate: "All Scripture is God inspired" (that is, God in-breathed). In other words, God's Holy Spirit filled the biblical authors, impressing them like a hot iron making a clear impression in soft wax, and what they wrote are the exact words that God wanted us to hear through the unique gifts of that particular writer; dead center, bull's-eye every time in the original text! Since then, every biblical scholar has tried to find the closest possible translation for that pure, original word. And keep in mind that, according to New Testament scholar Professor Tim Geddert, we know almost every word in the original Bible!

Speaking about the accuracy and purity of God's Word, King David says in Psalm 12:6, "The words of the Lord are flawless, like silver refined in a furnace of clay, purified seven times" (NIV). An illustration given by John Stott at an international meeting of evangelists in Amsterdam in 2000 shows the reverence Christians must have for the Bible.

> A soldier is on duty on the war front, and has in his pocket a picture of his beloved fiancée thousands of miles away. Whenever he has some peace of mind, he gently pulls out the picture of his loved one back home. He carefully studies her smile and her beautiful lips, and the beauty of her hair and every wave and curl in it. Just before reverently putting the picture away, he kisses it gently with his lips. He knows this is not his beloved, but this picture brings him the very best memory and joy he can have without her.

Dr. Stott's point is well taken. Christians who love the Bible do not worship it, they worship God. Because of that worship, they are attentive to every word and detail they can gain from this picture of their beloved God and Father of the Lord Jesus Christ.

THE BIBLE AS EMPIRICAL KNOWLEDGE OF GOD

Where does the Bible get the immense authority to communicate God's personal conversation to people like T.V. Thomas, Tawfik George, St. Augustine, and us?

The Bible is the most powerful instrument on earth to bring God's presence into our contemporary world. Why? Because when we hear or see the words in the Bible, we enter an experience of God directly and fully in a propositional revelation—that is, we have a truth encounter! *God is fully experienced by believers reading the Bible*, and thence, it can be called empirical—proven by the experimentation of the physical senses. We directly experience God's own personal presence through these words filled with his own Holy Spirit!

Thus, we now see that faith is *not* blind faith, nor mere intuition, nor strong emotional feeling. Faith comes from experiencing God as he speaks through real, visible, empirical words. The Bible says of this experience: "Faith comes from hearing, and hearing through the word of Christ" (Romans 10:17, ESV). In hearing these words, we have the actual empirical experience of hearing God.

If it is true that God inspired (in-breathed) his words to the Bible authors by a full imparting of his Holy Spirit, then these words were to the authors and are to us immediate and direct contact with almighty God. God is not just a belief. Rather, the Christian God is empirical—received in our own experience. We directly experience something of God himself in the Word that he has given—whether it is a word that we read (experienced by sight) or a word that we hear. When we experience this exact Word in front of us and invite God to speak through it, we directly experience God through his words in the fullness of God's presence in his Holy Spirit!

When God created our first ancestors in paradise, God also created their original language. Other languages in the world since the time of the Tower of Babel, and their words, are vehicles created by humankind. They belong to the created, natural world.

Here we see that God is great enough that he can be understood and known interactively in a personal conversation with us, using human words that we understand, even though these languages themselves were created by human beings. God takes human words that belong to us as creatures and fills these words with his experienced presence.

God, to the Christian, is empirical, proven in the experience of hearing God speak in the Bible. God filled the minds of the prophets and apostles to receive his speech and to write it faithfully. In turn, what the reader receives in these human words is a divinely inspired Word again filled with God's presence, known as his Holy Spirit.

As human beings, we can either see the words in the Bible as the inspired words of a human author, as a human work, or we can actually experience the fullness of almighty God through hearing these words filled with the same Holy Spirit who guided the original writer.

This is not a God of blind faith, but the living God, seen and heard "through the living and enduring word of God" (1 Peter 1:23).

WHY DO SOME READERS NOT EXPERIENCE GOD IN THE BIBLE?

Much is said today about the inspiration of the Bible, yet often only as a human expression of human faith. In one sense, the Bible can be, and can remain, only an expression of the human author. Thus, the reader can see and understand the words, but not have any experience of God in those words.

We owe to the 1647 Westminster Confession of Faith the highest possible expression of the experience of hearing only human words in the Bible. The Westminster Confession comes from a time when William Shakespeare wrote his immortal poetry and plays, and it possesses the same eloquence found in Shakespeare:

> We may be moved and induced by the testimony of the Church to an high and reverent esteem of the holy scriptures, and the heavenliness of the matter, the efficacy of the doctrine, the majesty of the style, the consent of all the parts, the scope of the whole (which is to give all the glory to God), the full discovery it makes of the only way of man's salvation, the many other incomparable excellencies, and the entire perfection thereof, are arguments whereby it doth abundantly evidence itself to be the word of God; yet notwithstanding our full persuasion and assurance of the infallible truth, and divine authority thereof, *is from the inward work of the Holy Spirit, bearing witness by and with the word in our hearts* (emphasis mine).[49]

It was one of the greatest reformers, John Calvin, writing in *The Institutes of the Christian Religion* in 1542, who preceded the Westminster Confession's wisdom in writing about God's inner testimony in our hearts (a reality he termed, "testimonium internum Spiritu

Sancti"),[50] which is absolutely necessary if indeed we are to hear God speaking directly and personally to us in the Scriptures.

The reason the Scriptures have the title *The Holy Bible* is not because of any holiness of its authors, as good as they were as people, but because the book takes all its holiness from God, as through it the holy God speaks to the world. And unless we experience God personally in reading the Bible through the Holy Spirit's enabling, what Calvin termed "the internal testimony of the Holy Spirit," we will merely experience a human author—the Bible will be merely a human classic, no matter how inspiring.

There is a principle behind all theology that was spoken frequently by my former professor and the winner of the Templeton Prize in Religion, TF Torrance, at the University of Edinburgh. He emphasized, "Through God alone may God be known."[51]

I believe the honest seeker will always find God speaking to him or her in the Scriptures, but the reader must pass beyond all the superlatives of the Bible listed in the Westminster Confession and humbly ask God to speak personally through these—his own words—as the Confession concludes. It is always true: if you seek after God, human authors can help point you to God's Word in the Bible, but it is *God* you ultimately must hear and respond to, for "only through God can God be known."

A TESTIMONY: MR. COOPER'S CLASS

For me, high school brought a struggle between two beautiful extremes.

On the one hand stood the most inspiring teacher I have ever had in my life, Mr. N. Roy Clifton, who taught geography, was the school librarian, and both directed and produced the annual school play. Mr. Clifton's wife, Helen, assisted his work in the school, and his daughter, Janie, who was my age, was just as great an influence.

Mr. Clifton had graduated as a barrister-at-law but gave up practicing law because of what he sometimes saw as the unjust defense of the guilty. His high sense of ethics carried over into his strict vegetarianism, which he and his family faithfully observed.

The Cliftons felt closest spiritually to the Unitarians and the Society of Friends, although they were very eclectic in their flirtation with Wicca. Mr. Clifton's greatest admiration was for the pacifist Hindu Mahatma Gandhi, who brought independence to India from the British Empire through nonviolent demonstrations. I believe Mr. Clifton was basically agnostic about some traditional Christian beliefs, while leaning strongly toward Hindu beliefs in reincarnation and nirvana, where the human spirit is finally released into the ocean of God's spirit.

Our entire high school was inspired by Mr. and Mrs. Clifton. They regularly took students to the Toronto Symphony Orchestra's Concerts for Young People, initiated some of us in attending the ballets at the Royal Alexandria Theatre, began screening outstanding "Films of Note" at the local theater in Richmond Hill, and guided many students to begin a lifetime of reading.

Mr. Clifton's daughter, Janie, was a true Clifton in drawing the very best from people's raw potential. In grade eleven, Janie heard my speech in English class and somehow, despite my utter disbelief in my own ability, talked me into entering the oratorical contest at the school assembly. I didn't win the competition, but it gave me an entirely new confidence in speaking before large crowds.

This success led Janie to persuade me to read for a part in the school play that same year, and I ended up taking the leading roles in plays over the next two years. In grade thirteen, I took a minor role because of my academic workload. That last year, a young actor in grade nine took an interest in our school drama club and has become over the years one of Canada's best-known actors. His name—R.H. Thompson.

Another significant person who entered my life as I began high school was the Reverend Jack Cooper. When Jack moved into our community of Maple, attending our local church, he served as National Director of Church Extension at the denominational headquarters in Toronto in an unprecedented era of population and construction growth in Canadian cities and the planting of new churches. Mr. Cooper's wife, Helen, was our organist and choir director, and Mr. Cooper began a young people's Bible study which I and my younger sister Marilyn attended.

Mr. Cooper and Mr. Clifton were two dynamic lightning rods who directed powerful bolts of emotional and intellectual energy into my young life. This dialectic of opposites created a powerful movement of questions from my school life to answers in Mr. Cooper's Bible study class.

Everything you could ask about God and related issues—the Trinity, Jesus Christ, miracles, the authority of the Bible, and other religions; ethical issues like celibacy, ecology, and abortion; and even political questions like communism—was vigorously debated in Mr. Cooper's Bible study class. And the framework against which these questions were answered was a study of the Gospel of Luke and then the Acts of the Apostles. It was incredible that what at first appeared as insoluble questions in the richness of my high school life could be so satisfyingly and adequately answered by Mr. Cooper from the Christian Bible. I longed to share with as many of my generation as possible this Good News I was hearing from the Bible. I was beginning to realize that God was starting to place a call upon my life as both a pastor and an evangelist.

Richmond Hill High School is now closed, but for many years it had the highest or second-highest ratings of all the public high schools in Ontario. I am very grateful for the immense stimulation it gave me to question my world, but even greater was the deep satisfaction I found in attending Mr. Cooper's Bible study to seek and find answers in God's Word.

THE HEART OF THE SCRIPTURES

We now turn to the very center of the entire Bible in its two thousand years of history, a center that I discovered in Mr. Cooper's Bible study class: the beating heart of our best knowledge of God in the life, death, and resurrection of the Lord Jesus Christ.

The body of rational knowledge of God given in Jesus Christ began the first science of God in all the cultures of the world—*theology*, called in seminaries "the queen of the sciences." Nor did it stop there. This rational knowledge of God in Jesus Christ inspired the first steps toward what we now know as the investigative, rational sciences of the natural world. Not only is the bank of theologians sitting at the peak of the highest mountain, but they're at its base as well! Like the Roman procurator, Pontius Pilate, we may all have some knowledge of Jesus. When Jesus finally stood before this Roman official at his trial, Pilate said, *"Ecce Homo!"*—"Behold, the man!" Let us behold the Master ourselves in the next four chapters.

CHAPTER 4
A Conversation
with Jesus

The case for Jesus is the most vulnerable point, the potential Achilles' heel, of the Christian faith and in the human search for the living God. If Jesus Christ of Nazareth can offer accurate, reliable knowledge of God, then we will find our search for the living God answered! If Jesus cannot provide us with necessary, sufficient, and reliable knowledge of God, then what credibility is left for finding God in our human history?

The greatest twentieth-century Christian theologian, Karl Barth, observed that Jesus is the "datum" for all our knowledge of God and provides the factual evidence for all true theology. Barth observed this throughout all his many volumes of the *Church Dogmatics*, in which he expressed the theological science of knowing God in the positive revelation of Jesus Christ.[52] If theology lacks credible knowledge of the "historical Jesus," then surely all Christian thinking about God is in peril.

Recently, great doubt has been cast on the idea of finding the real, "historical" Jesus by a group of religious thinkers called The Jesus Seminar. Wikipedia summarizes:

> A group of about one hundred and fifty critical scholars and laymen have met calling themselves The Jesus Seminar founded in 1985 by Robert Funk and John Dominic Crossan under the auspices of the Westar Institute. The seminar uses votes with colored beads to decide their collective view of the historicity of the deeds and sayings of Jesus of Nazareth.[53]

This group's notoriety in denying many words that Jesus spoke and the deeds he did has been heightened by numerous newspaper feature writers who boldly inform North American readers again and again that, based on the seminar's fringe work, "scholars" no longer believe in the Jesus of the Bible. The controversy is reflected in books by John Crossan and Marcus Borg and is intensified by the media's frenzied reporting.

To answer doubts from The Jesus Seminar, and also criticism from atheists like Dawkins, we will now examine the record of Jesus Christ in the most reliable words he taught (chapter 4), the most credible deeds he carried out (chapter 5), the meaning of his death (chapter 6), and the claims for his resurrection (chapter 7). We will examine the question of eternal life in chapter 8, completing this section on "God in History."

In earlier chapters, we began our search for God in nature, and we have now moved from the natural world to history—real history in space and time. But how can we best answer the question of who the historical Jesus is?

Questions as to who Jesus truly is aren't new. Even during the years of Jesus's ministry, the disciples themselves must have asked these questions over and over again! Who is this Jesus, where did he come from, what is he trying to do? It may help us to ask how Jesus's disciples arrived at their answer to who Jesus was—was he a powerful prophet like those we find in the Old Testament, an inspiring rabbi, a great holy high priest, or even a royal king? What drove them to their beliefs in Jesus?

The answer is extremely important for us in the twenty-first century, because we discover the true identity of Jesus in exactly the same way his first disciples did. There were three very reliable ways for the early disciples, and for us too, to find accurate knowledge of the historical Jesus:

(1) By identifying the most historically reliable words that Jesus spoke.
(2) By coming to a reasonable understanding of the deeds he did, and very importantly.
(3) By listening to the statements of witnesses in the Bible about who Jesus was to them.

We will begin our discovery of who Jesus is in this section, by identifying the most authentic words that the historical Jesus spoke.

JESUS—JUST ANOTHER MYTHOLOGY?

Is the story of Jesus in the Bible just another mythology? According to some recent popular books, like *The Pagan Christ* by Canadian author Tom Harpur, the Bible is a collection of myths coming from ancient civilizations that were rewritten for biblical audiences.[54] Is Jesus just another mythology, or does he bring us factual, historical evidence for an accurate knowledge of God?

So much of what makes up the other religions in the world is *not* science or factual, but instead is only fanciful mythology. Some of the earliest religions from the first great civilizations have been mythological, such as in the cultures of Babylon, Egypt, Greece, and Rome—great world empires with elaborate mythological belief systems. Almost everyone today sees these early religions as elaborate fictions buttressed by magnificent temples, flourishing in classical antiquity and expressed in writings about the incredible exploits of their all-too-human mythological gods.

So is there a truly "historical Jesus," or is he just another early mythology?

Distressingly, it is not just authors like Tom Harpur and Dan Brown (*The Da Vinci Code*) who link Christianity with mythology. For example, when one visits the ancient city of Rome, the historical and cultural epicenter of Christianity, it may haunt the tourist to find that Christianity could appear to be just another mythology supplanting the older mythologies of pagan Rome.

For example, many of the Egyptian and Roman mythologies had fathers, mothers, and sons. These essential Christian themes of Father, Mother, and Son are found everywhere in Christian Rome. One of the Vatican's greatest artists, Michelangelo, was deeply impressed with the ancient sculptures of Roman gods in the Vatican collection. In later life, when Michelangelo was turning blind, he would hug the ancient torso of Hercules with its massive thighs and waist, which had influenced the physiques of his earlier sculptures. Michelangelo was a sincerely devout Christian artist with knowledge of the Bible, but his work was imbued with the inspiration of classical antiquity.

One of Michelangelo's greatest works, *The Last Judgment* on the back wall of the Sistine Chapel (where the conclave of Roman Catholic cardinals chooses a new pope), displays a most beautiful face for the Lord Jesus. Michelangelo copied it directly from the face of an ancient sculpture of Apollo that was created in pagan times and is now housed in the Vatican Museum. Has Jesus taken on the appearance of a new kind of Apollo, a sun god? The setting sun is even included in this scene.

Another example connects to this: the birth of Jesus, the Son of God, is celebrated on December 25 in the Christian West. This is also the date of the winter solstice of earlier pagan times, when Apollo was thought to begin his rebirth as the sun god across the heavens.

Or view the oldest and most impressive pagan temple in Rome, the high-domed Pantheon, built decades before the birth of Jesus as a temple to honor and worship all the ancient Roman gods. The pagan images have all now been removed and replaced by Christian statues and altars to the Christian God.

One might even hear from a tour guide at the Vatican Museum or while visiting the Coliseum or the Palatine Hill that the guide feels as much a member of pagan, mythological Rome as he does of modern-day Catholic Rome!

All of this is disturbing. Are we perilously close to closing our eyes to the historical Jesus and closing our Bibles as a source of reliable knowledge of God?

After all, we are not here to study mythology. Even though we may be persuaded of God by personal experience or believe in God as the First Cause or Intelligent Designer of the universe, we want to know where in our *real world* we can find additional facts and rational knowledge of God. If only we could study God in some rational, physical way, as the natural sciences of biology and physics do in their experiments in nature!

Well, perhaps we can. I hope to establish in this chapter the "physical" knowledge of God as revealed to the disciples in the New Testament, who claimed to have seen and heard the *truly human* Jesus Christ—who, as they wrote, "has dwelt among us, and we have seen His glory, glory as of the only Son from the Father, full of grace and truth" (John 1:14, ESV). Nor does this happen outside of human history. The Christian events are located in a historical continuum, with biblical events identified by other secular events of the day (i.e. Luke 2:1–3).

The disciples saw God in a tangible, physical way in what can be called "the humanity of God." Their testimony takes us far beyond any question of the Bible as mythology: it is something else indeed, something firmly standing as factual evidence for our rational, even empirical, knowledge of God. Jesus said to an unbelieving disciple, "Whoever has seen me has seen the Father" (John 14: 9). In Jesus, we see what the Bible calls the visible "image of the invisible God" (Colossians 1:15, ESV). In seeing Jesus, we see God. Hopefully the reader will also discover that in Jesus Christ, seeing is believing!

GOD'S PROMISE IN THE OLD TESTAMENT

Jesus comes within the context of the Bible, part of which, the Old Testament, had already been written before his lifetime.

The first half of the Christian Bible, the Old Testament, has as its dominant theme the story of God calling Abraham, Isaac, Jacob, and their ancestors, the Jews, to be his covenant people, carrying God's Word to all the nations of the earth. Moses was their greatest prophet, living about 1440 BC, whom God called to deliver the Jews from their slavery in Egypt into the promised land of Canaan. Under Moses, the children of Israel spent forty years in the wilderness before entering the promised land under the prophet Joshua.

Then, for several hundred years Israel was led by judges (military leaders). Around 1025 BC, the Jews demanded of God that they be made like the other nations around them and have their own king to lead them and administer the affairs of the nation. Saul was their first king, followed by King David. As their anointed leader, David became the greatest king in all of the Old Testament.

David was a brilliant military general and the talented author of many psalms (poetry praising God) whom God called a man after his own heart (see 1 Samuel 13:14). David also founded the city of Jerusalem, which still stands today in the same location and with the same name as when it began in 1000 BC. A royal sarcophagus has been found recently in Jerusalem which many Jews believe today to be the burial casket of King David. It can be seen by tourists in the Old City.[55]

Under David and his successor, King Solomon, Israel won her greatest dominance over the surrounding nations in all the history of the Jewish people. Hence, the Jews cherished the promise God had given to David that from David's offspring there would come the ultimate Savior-King, one who would usher in the reign of God forever. God renewed this promise to all Israel through many of the prophets, priests, and kings of that time and later, up to the time of the birth of Jesus Christ. The nation longed for the anointed son of David, who would be born to fulfill God's promise of salvation and effect the redemption of Israel and the world!

No one spoke more of the anointed Messianic King to come than the prophet Isaiah. One of Israel's greatest prophets, Isaiah wrote as one of the most literary authors in the Old Testament. The copy of the book of Isaiah has been found in perfect condition among the Dead Sea scrolls in the mid-twentieth century, almost exactly word-for-word matching our most modern Hebrew Bible. Isaiah wrote in the period c. 740–681 BC.

At the time of Isaiah, the Jews had never had a greater need for God's anointed king to come. The Northern Kingdom of Israel had just fallen to the Assyrians, and God had revealed through Isaiah and many other prophets that the Southern Kingdom, Judah, would be defeated next. In these desperate times, God raised up major and minor prophets to encourage the despairing chosen people of God that the Messianic Son of David would certainly come. Here is God's promise to suffering Israel through the prophet Isaiah:

The people who walked in *darkness* have seen a great *light*;
those who lived in a land of deep darkness—
on them *light has shined* . . .

For a child has been born for us,
a son given to us;
authority rests on his shoulders;
and he is named
Wonderful Counselor, Mighty God,
Everlasting Father, Prince of Peace.
His authority shall grow continually,
and there shall be endless peace
for the throne of David and his kingdom.

He will establish and uphold it
with justice and with righteousness
from this time onward and forevermore.
The zeal of the Lord of hosts will do this. (Isaiah 9:2,6–7, emphasis mine)

As splendid as the primordial first day of creation, the time for the birth of the Messiah finally came! According to the biblical account, around 1 BC, a Jewish maiden named Mary, of the lineage of King David, gave birth to a son in King David's hometown of Bethlehem—and the Light promised in Isaiah and in several hundred other Old Testament prophecies finally shone in all its brilliance—first locally, to shepherds in the field, then distantly, to the wise men from the east, and later, in Jesus's adult life, as "the Light of the world" (John 8:12).

The world asks the Christian: "How do you know all this is true?"

THINGS THE HISTORICAL JESUS SAID

To readers of contemporary newspapers, it may appear hopeless to expect any reliable information in the New Testament about Jesus. As has already been noted, much news in the media in the last decade about The Jesus Seminar and its overcritical search for "the historical Jesus" has helped decay the faith for many. These scholars assume a very critical attitude in their distrusting examination of the Holy Bible. Overzealous feature writers in newspapers have jumped on the bandwagon to question the historicity of the New Testament record on Jesus.

This isn't the first attempt to find the "real Jesus" embedded somewhere in Scripture—it is actually the third attempt by New Testament scholars in the last one hundred and fifty years to penetrate and dissect the biblical text for what they have thought to be the most accurate and reliable knowledge about the real, historical Jesus, in a critical attempt to shear away from the text what they feel are layers of "exaggeration," "contradiction" and just plain "mythology."

Because of the prevalence of such ideas, let us make an attempt to unravel the historical Jesus and deal with doubts about the biblical text by some contemporary scholars, even using some of their own methodology.

First, where can we find the most likely reliable words the historical Jesus spoke? As some of these questioning scholars would say, the place to start here is to find what could be *the most easily remembered words* Jesus taught.

JESUS'S MOST MEMORABLE WORDS

There is no better place to start than with the parables of Jesus, which are so uniquely memorable—fictional short stories like the parables of the Good Samaritan, the Prodigal Son, the Tax Collector and the Pharisee, and the Sower. They are so vivid in their telling and clear in their spiritual meaning that many in Jesus's day would never forget them! They would be the easiest and most accurate memories of Jesus's words to record.

However, there is still another group of memorable words from Jesus which are just as reliable as the parables. They are on the same level as his teachings in the parables, and just as unique to Jesus, so they may stand the test as coming from the historical Jesus. These other teachings are found in Jesus's Sermon on the Mount, as we read it in Matthew 5, 6, and 7, as well as in the other gospels, especially Luke 6:17–49. These teachings are as grand, unusual, and therefore uniquely characteristic of Jesus as his parables. Moreover, these words would be so extremely easy to memorize and so highly useful in the preaching of his first disciples during and after Jesus's ministry on earth that they must also be attributable directly to Jesus.

The apostle Matthew, who wrote the first biography of Jesus we read in the New Testament, was a tax collector who may have recorded some of Jesus's words verbatim on his tax tablet with chalk, but most of Jesus's other disciples had to rely on memory and would remember most vividly the fictional parables and outstanding teachings Jesus gave as found throughout the Sermon on the Mount.

JESUS'S SERMON ON THE MOUNT

The Sermon on the Mount is so unique to Jesus and so unusual that it has impressed many world leaders, even of other faiths. Mahatma Gandhi, the Hindu lawyer who brought independence to India from Britain in the twentieth century, read the entire Sermon on the Mount every day of his life and drew from its teachings his inspiration for nonviolent political victory for India. These lofty teachings are consistent with everything else that is so unique in the New Testament about Jesus as a teacher! But there is more, much more, that we can learn from the words of the Sermon on the Mount than that they are the exceptional world-quality teachings of a great spiritual master.

If we accept the Sermon on the Mount as the historical words of Jesus, we can then ask and answer this significant question: "What do these words in the Sermon on the Mount tell us about who *Jesus* said he was?"

POPE BENEDICT'S BOOK ON JESUS

There is a most remarkable and enlightening book on the life of Jesus Christ called *Jesus of Nazareth*[56] by Pope Benedict XVI, published in 2007. "This book," Pope Benedict writes, "is my personal search 'for the face of the Lord.'" It is filled with insight into traditional and contemporary interpretations of the Lord Jesus Christ with an extreme rigor to be faithful to the biblical accounts of the Lord.

In a long chapter on the Sermon on the Mount, Pope Benedict notes the similarities and differences between Jesus and Moses, who both went up on the mount to teach the people the Law of God, called in Hebrew the Torah.

The Bible says that Moses was a humble and faithful human instrument of the Lord to transmit the Torah as God mediated it through him. Moses clearly declared that he was neither the law nor the Lawgiver—God alone did that. Moses stands only as God's servant in reporting the Torah God transmitted through him for Israel, as we see in Deuteronomy:

> You must neither add anything to what I command you nor take away anything from it, but keep the command of the Lord your God with which I am charging you . . . See, just as the Lord my God has charged me, I

now teach you statutes and ordinances for you to observe in the land that you are about to enter and occupy. (Deuteronomy 4:2, 5)

Similarly, Jesus climbed the hills of Galilee as a teacher, but he taught the people a new Torah from himself. Unlike Moses, Jesus is not a human mediator for God, but stands in the place of God himself in pronouncing Jesus's new Torah. Unlike Moses, Jesus stands as both the new Torah and the Lawgiver!

You have heard it said in ancient times, "You shall not commit murder . . . But I say to you . . . " (Matthew 5:21–22)

Again, you have heard that it was said to those of ancient times, "You shall not swear falsely . . . But I say to you . . . " (Matthew 5:33–34)

You have heard it said, "An eye for an eye and a tooth for a tooth." But I say unto you "Do not resist an evildoer. But if anyone strikes you on the right cheek, turn the other also . . . " (Matthew 5:38–39)

The crowds were stunned by these words and teachings of Jesus. On a number of occasions, as on this, the Gospels record that "when Jesus had finished saying these things, the crowds were astounded at his teachings, for he taught them as one having authority, and not as their scribes" (Matthew 7:28–29).

If these are the memorable and unique words of the Lord Jesus, then who is this man? Surely the crowds were asking themselves this question, and the disciples too!

A JEW'S CONVERSATION WITH JESUS

There is a poignant section in Pope Benedict's book that I would like to quote at length. The Pontiff is fascinated with a Jewish scholar, Rabbi Jacob Neusner, who wrote a book called *A Rabbi Talks with Jesus*. Rabbi Neusner grew up with Christians and Jews and is very respectfully attracted to Jesus while remaining with the "eternal Israel." In Neusner's book, he places himself in the time of Jesus and engages in a personal discussion with Jesus, just as if he were a contemporary of the Lord traveling with him through Galilee. After spending the day with Jesus, Neusner sojourns for the night with the Jews of that place and consults the local rabbi. Neusner writes the following dialogue, as quoted by Pope Benedict:

> The rabbi cites from the Babylonian Talmud:
>
> Rabbi Simelai expounded: "Six hundred and thirteen commandments were given to Moses, three hundred and sixty-five negative ones, corresponding to the number of days of the solar year, and two hundred forty-eight positive commandments, corresponding to the parts of man's body,
>
> "David came and reduced them to eleven . . .
>
> "Isaiah came and reduced them to six . . .
>
> "Isaiah again came and reduced them to two . . .
>
> "Habakkuk further came and based them on one, as it is said: 'but the righteous shall live by his faith.'" (Hab 2:4)
>
> Neusner then continues his book with the following dialogue: "So," the master says, "is this what the sage Jesus had to say?"
>
> I: "Not exactly, but close."
>
> He: "What did he leave out?"
>
> I: "Nothing."
>
> He: "Then what did he add?"
>
> I: "Himself."[57]

Pope Benedict observes, "This is the central point where the believing Jew Neusner experiences alarm at Jesus' message, and this is the central reason why he does not wish to follow Jesus, but remains with the 'eternal Israel': the centrality of Jesus 'I' in his message, which gives everything a new direction."

The pope continues, "It is only with great respect and reverence that Neusner addresses this mysterious identification of Jesus and God that is in the discourses of the Sermon on the Mount. Nevertheless, his analysis shows that this is the point where Jesus' message diverges fundamentally from the faith of the 'eternal Israel.'"[58]

Rabbi Neusner observes how Jesus puts himself in the place of God in the Sermon on the Mount. Jesus speaks as the Lawgiver and as the Law himself. Pope Benedict gives, once more, a great insight into Jesus's identity as Lawgiver and as God:

> The issue that is really at the heart of the debate is thus finally laid bare. Jesus understands Himself as the Torah—as the word of God in person. The tremendous prologue of John's Gospel—'In the beginning was the Word, and the Word was with God, and the Word was God' (John 1:1)—says nothing different from what Jesus of the Sermon on the Mount and the Jesus of the Synoptic Gospels says. The Jesus of the fourth Gospel and the Jesus of the Synoptic is one and the same: the true "historical" Jesus.[59]

The Jewish Rabbi Neusner recognizes the teachings of the Sermon on the Mount as legitimately coming from Jesus, who in the Sermon on the Mount identifies himself as equal to God the Father as God's unique Son. The rabbi can recognize and react to Jesus in this teaching in the same way many of the Jewish religious leaders did at the time, rejecting Jesus's claims as God and staying with the "eternal Israel." As Pope Benedict concludes, Rabbi Neusner's debate gives the grounds for us to know the "historical Jesus"!

What about this "egotism" of Jesus in the Sermon on the Mount presenting himself as both the Lawgiver and the new Holy Torah himself? Do we find this in the other gospels?

In the Gospel of John, Jesus's extensive egotism can be found in the major "I Am" statements spoken by Jesus: "I am the Light of the world"—"I am the Bread of Life"—"I am the Resurrection and the Life"—"I am the way, the truth, and the life"—"I am the Good Shepherd."[60] What were the Jewish authorities to think when Jesus made these personal references to himself as the great "I am," when the most reverenced name for God in the Old Testament is *Yahweh*, "I am who I am"?

Thus, the earliest and most reliable record of Jesus's teachings reveals that Jesus presented himself as God the Son. This *is* the original, historical Jesus. And as God, Jesus satisfies our quest for knowledge of the hidden God of creation and design!

The disciples must have struggled intensely with these teachings of Jesus, since as good Jews they believed in the One God who was wholly apart from the sinful world of humanity and its fallen state. And in fact, at one point in Jesus's teachings we hear that many of Jesus's disciples stopped traveling with him and believing in him when his teaching became too offensive for them: "Because of this many of his disciples turned back and no longer went about with him" (John 6:60 and 66). Some could not stomach the fact that Jesus made himself identical to their Holy One of Israel! Jesus's words were truly "sharper than any two-edged sword" (Hebrews 4:12), offending some, but "words of life" to a world waiting to see and hear from the hidden God!

Given the difficulty of his teachings, we have to ask: did Jesus's inner circle of the twelve apostles also want to leave him? The impetuous spokesman for the twelve, Peter, answered for them all:

> So Jesus asked the twelve, "Do you also wish to go away?" Simon Peter answered Him, "Lord, to whom can we go? You have the words of eternal life. We have come to believe and know that You are the Holy One of God." (John 6:67–69)

For Peter and the twelve, Jesus's words were not just the profound teaching of a great national rabbi. They opened the very doors of heaven. Just as in the classic story in the Old Testament of angels ascending and descending from heaven upon the newly blessed Jacob, Israel's founder, Jesus's words led to the very entrance to the gates of heaven and into eternal life.

Nevertheless, Jesus's words are not just for eternity, but apply directly to this present world: "I came that they may have life, and have it abundantly" (John 10:10). The apostles were intoxicated by the Master's words of immortality and by the inner exultation they felt in this world while following him!

The teachings in the Sermon on the Mount, coming from the historical Jesus, paint an icon of the Master so we can understand Jesus's words when he said to Philip, "If you have seen me, you have seen the Father" (John 14:9). Jesus painted his own self-portrait in the Sermon on the Mount and verbally confirmed that picture in several key encounters.

Consider Jesus's encounter with the Samaritan woman at the well at Sychar, where she had come to draw water. Jesus initiated a conversation about giving her "living water," and shared a powerful and personal conversation with her about her past five husbands. She searched in her mind for a description of this perceptive Jewish teacher:

> The woman said to Him, "I know that Messiah is coming (He who is called Christ); when that One comes, He will declare all things to us." Jesus said to her, "I am He, the one who is speaking to you." (John 4:25–26)

Again, the icon Jesus paints of himself is of the Jewish Messiah, the prophesied Savior-King promised to come into the world by Isaiah and many others in the Old Testament.

Words, in the biographies of Jesus in the New Testament, are signposts of the invisible God, spoken by the Lord Jesus Christ, the Son of God. However, because words can disguise the truth and be counterfeits of reality, people often find that what someone *does* counts for so much more than what they merely *say*. Can this be the case with Jesus? What, in history, did he *do*?

We now turn to our chapter on Jesus's deeds and the testimony his disciples gave to him, where we will look to see if his deeds are just as authoritative as his words in revealing the true, historical Jesus and the heavenly Father.

CHAPTER 5
The Big Question: Things Jesus Did

Jesus's disciples discovered the true Jesus not only through the authoritative words he spoke, but just as much through the things he did. What reliable knowledge do we have of what Jesus did?

Nestled on a hilltop above the Sea of Galilee in the Holy Land is the picturesque Church of the Beatitudes. This location, or somewhere near here, could be where Jesus gave his Sermon on the Mount, and it makes a great place to read portions of this teaching. Tourists visiting here today are struck by Jesus's words in much the same way as his original listeners probably were. "Who is this man?" they ask themselves. His teachings strongly trace Jesus back to God, whom he called his Father. However, he did not expect his disciples to accept this identity based on his words alone. There were many things that Jesus *did* that helped his disciples discover the true identity of their Master and Lord.

Let us leave the Church of the Beatitudes and travel the winding road down to the lakeside town of Capernaum. It is now just ruins, devastated over the centuries by recurring earthquakes. But we do find here the remains of a first-century synagogue, probably the same one Jesus preached and healed in, since this was the home base for his ministry around the Sea of Galilee. Clergy visiting here often weep, knowing they are possibly standing on the very same pavement their Lord did two millennia earlier. And it is here we discover that it was not just the words Jesus spoke that made him Lord and Savior. Just as much, it was the miracles Jesus performed. They were signs given to the crowds to know who Jesus was.

A VISIT WITH JESUS, THE GREAT PHYSICIAN

A remarkable incident in Capernaum revealed Jesus as God in both word and deed. It occurred in a home there. The story is found in Mark 2, near the beginning of the shortest and possibly the earliest of the four Gospels to be written.

In the story, Jesus is teaching, and crowds crush into the house. More people gathered outside within hearing distance. A miracle is about to happen. Men come carrying a paralyzed friend on his pallet, wanting to place this invalid before the Great Physician. But their way is blocked by the jam of listeners all around the house. One of them finds steps to the roof of the house, and he brings the others up with him. They remove the convertible portion of the roof, used possibly for ventilation. They find ropes there, so they fasten the pallet to the ropes and lower the man down in front of the Master below. The crowd is stunned by this, and they wait to see and hear what Jesus will do. "When Jesus saw their faith," Mark records, "he said to the paralytic, 'Son, your sins are forgiven'" (Mark 2:5).

Now, these are strange words to hear from any human being. Jesus perceived that this man's greatest need, far greater even than walking again, was the forgiveness of his sins. And he bestowed that forgiveness out of his own unique position of authority. None of the significance of these words was lost to the religious authorities, the Pharisees, who immediately questioned in their hearts who could forgive sins but God alone. Again, this is another account of Jesus's teachings landing him in the place of God. The authorities thought so and were deeply offended! Even Jesus's disciples must have asked themselves, "Who does this man think he is?"

But it wasn't just the words Jesus spoke that helped the crowds to answer this existential question. It was also what he did.

> At once Jesus perceived in his spirit that they were discussing these questions among themselves; and he said to them, "Why do you raise such questions in your hearts? Which is easier to say to the paralytic, 'Your sins are forgiven,' or to say, 'Stand up and take your mat and walk'? But so that you may know that the Son of Man has authority on earth to forgive sins"—he said to the paralytic—"I say to you, stand up, take your mat and go to your home." And he stood up, and immediately took the mat and went out before all of them. (Mark 2:8–12)

All the miracles Jesus performed were signs to the people that One greater than all the prophets was with them. Many prophets performed great miracles—like Elijah calling down fire from heaven or raising a dead boy—but all the prophets were servants of God, displaying God's power, not their own human power or ability. Jesus did many miracles, like the prophets, but he did them in his own name and by his own authority as God himself. That's why the Pharisees murmured their discontent when Jesus healed the paralytic: because it was not just the work of a prophet, but the work of God himself to heal and also to forgive sins. His miraculous deeds were signs and wonders that brought faith to the crowds that Jesus was identical to God—just as his teachings did! To give a miracle of healing is just as great as for God to forgive sins. Both are works of God. Jesus's healings are as great a revelation of God's power and presence as his authoritative words.

THE CREATOR CREATING WINE

Another great miracle is worth mentioning here. It is found in John 2, in which Jesus performed his first miracle at a wedding feast in Cana of Galilee, not far from Jesus's hometown of Nazareth. The steward of the banquet ran out of wine early in the celebration, and Jesus's mother, Mary, came to Jesus to tell him, "They have no wine." Jesus resisted for a moment but then took charge.

"Fill the jars with water . . . Now draw some out, and take it to the chief steward." When the steward tasted the water turned into wine he exclaimed, "Everyone serves the good wine first, and then the inferior wine after the guests have become drunk. But you have kept the good wine until now." (John 2:1–11)

Like the combined healing and forgiveness of the paralytic in Capernaum, this miracle reveals Jesus to be God by the actions he performed. Water is completely different chemically from wine. Just as God created the universe out of nothing, as recorded in Genesis 1, so Jesus here acts as the Creator, making wine out of something physically different! Remember, Jesus's miraculous deeds were signs and wonders designed to specifically help seekers to know who he was. Here is the concluding verse in this account of Scripture: "Jesus did this, the first of his signs, in Cana of Galilee, and revealed his glory; and his disciples believed in him" (John 2:11).

His words as well as his deeds reveal to his disciples who Jesus is. Jesus always intended that someday his disciples would know who he was: God's Son, sent from the Father, born *Immanuel*, meaning "God with us." Do we find this kind of faith in Jesus from his disciples?

THINGS JESUS'S FOLLOWERS SAID ABOUT HIM

We've looked at what Jesus said and did, but there is a third thing to consider when we ask the question of whether Jesus was God come into history. What did those closest to Jesus say about him? As the disciples traveled with Jesus around the Sea of Galilee, they heard his authoritative words and saw his miraculous signs and wonders over about a three-year period. Impressions were forming. Faith was building. They asked themselves the same questions that everyone hearing Jesus asked and puzzled over, especially the authorities who questioned him: who was he, and "by what authority are you doing these things?" (Luke 20:2).

Finally, Jesus confronted their questions. The day of decision had finally come! Jesus took his disciples with him to where the Jordan River empties into the Sea of Galilee, then up this icy river to where it begins, bubbling up out of the ground at Israel's highest mountain, Mount Hermon. There you will find a small settlement called Caesarea Philippi. In this refreshing, inspirational setting, Jesus confronted his followers with this quintessential question:

"Who do people say that the Son of Man is?"

The disciples must have discussed this many times with various people in the crowds, being very perplexed themselves. They might have talked about Jesus being the "Light" prophesied by Isaiah, or the anointed "Messianic" descendant of King David, or even the coming "Immanuel."

But on this day at Caesarea Philippi, Jesus's disciples finally declared their faith. They began by relating the answers of the crowds:

"Some say John the Baptist, but others Elijah, and still others Jeremiah or one of the prophets."

Then Jesus asked his followers the existential question. Through them, Jesus addresses this question to the entire world!

"But who do *you say* that I am?"

Simon Peter, the impetuous and impulsive leader of this small group, stepped forward and dared to confess to Jesus, "You are the Messiah, the Son of the Living God" (see Matthew 16:13–16 for the whole conversation).

Peter recognized Jesus as the Old Testament Messiah, but also as the New Testament Second Person of the Triune God, "the Son of the living God," possibly shattering all the categories the disciples three years earlier had held as strict Jewish monotheists! Peter's answer not only placed him first and foremost among the twelve apostles, but became the ageless confession of faith for every believer in Jesus ever since. Upon this disciple, and this confession of faith, Jesus said that he would build his church.

FOLLOWING PETER'S FAITH

Others in the group came to the same conclusion as Peter did at different times. Philip, frustrated and perplexed by the Lord's teachings near the end of his ministry, bluntly asked him, "Lord, show us the Father and we will be satisfied." Jesus answered, "I am the way, and the truth, and the life. No one comes to the Father except through me. If you know me, you will know my Father also. From now on you do know him and have seen him" (John 14:6–8).

On another occasion, the disciple who has given his name to history as the archetypal doubter, the questioning Thomas, wasn't with the fledgling group of believers when Jesus first appeared alive after his crucifixion. Thomas told the other believers that he wouldn't believe this nonsense about a risen Lord unless he saw and physically touched the Savior. Within days, Jesus returned to this band hiding in the upper room, showed Thomas the wounds in his hands and side, and told him to touch and see for himself. Doubting Thomas could only fall to his knees before the physical, risen Lord and confess, like Peter, "My Lord and my God!" (John 20:28).

Others in the New Testament agreed to this confession of faith in Jesus. In about 56 AD, the apostle Paul, writing to the church he had helped found in the cosmopolitan Greek city of Corinth, wrote these words in his autobiographical second letter to them:

> For what we proclaim is not ourselves, but Jesus Christ as Lord, with ourselves as your servants for Jesus' sake. For God who said, "Let light shine out of darkness," has shone in our hearts to give the light of the knowledge of the glory of God in the face of Jesus Christ. (2 Corinthians 4:5–6, ESV)

The God I discovered in Sunday school at eleven years of age can be discovered and known so much better in the Bible than he could ever be as the First Cause of the cosmos discovered only in nature. The God who said at creation "Let light shine out of darkness" shines today, as Paul said, in the person of Jesus Christ. True knowledge of God comes not simply from recognizing him as the First Cause of all existing things, but from learning of the birth of Jesus in our historical world—God coming to us in a way we can understand. The apostle John wrote in his first letter:

> What was from the beginning, what we have heard, what we have seen with our eyes, what we have looked at and touched with our hands . . . we have seen and testify and proclaim to you. (1 John 1:1, 2)

God has from the beginning of the world been interactive, as the Bible records and as I humbly discovered one night from a shooting star. "The glory of God in the face of Jesus" that Paul speaks of is not found in the color of his skin or the color of his eyes, but is visible to the eyes of faith; it is a glory that "shines in our hearts." This is the internal testimony of the Holy Spirit, humbly seen and heard in the life of the Lord Jesus Christ. It shone in the hearts of those who watched him. It still shines in the hearts of those who sincerely and openly consider his claims today.

Even stronger superlatives can be found elsewhere in the New Testament, revealing the glory of Jesus as he reveals God to us. In the letter to the Hebrews 1:3 (ESV), we read:

> Jesus is the radiance of the glory of God and the exact imprint of his nature, and he upholds the universe by the word of his power.

The Creator has unveiled his glory in the face of Jesus Christ as he promised he would in the words of the Bible through the prophets, priests, and kings of the Old Testament. When God wanted to speak his long, personal, and intimate conversation with us, he spoke it into the flesh of his Son Jesus Christ: "And the Word became flesh and dwelt among us, and we have seen his glory, glory as of the only Son from the Father, full of grace and truth" (John 1:14, ESV).

THE CONTROVERSY CONTINUES!

Jesus's question, "Who do you say that I am?", and the apostolic answer to it in 33 AD, resonated throughout the bitter battles in the struggling church over the next three hundred years. The authors of the Bible provided all the ammunition for this battle, but it was only by intense study of the authentic apostolic books written in the first century (the full canon of the New Testament was acknowledged by about 150 AD) that the church fathers finally agreed to an ecumenical statement of faith, the Nicene Creed, confirmed by an almost unanimous meeting of the bishops in 315 AD. In it the apostolic fathers confessed their faith in God the Father, God the Son (Jesus Christ), and God the Holy Spirit after almost three hundred years of intense debate.

The Nicene Creed summarized all the main beliefs about almighty God that the Christian church found in the Scriptures and sought to preserve and proclaim. It is still a concise and powerful summary of what Christians find in the Bible to answer the quest for the living God:

We believe in one God,
the Father, the Almighty,
maker of heaven and earth,
of all that is, seen and unseen.

We believe in one Lord, Jesus Christ,
the only son of God,
eternally begotten of the Father,
God from God, Light from Light,
true God from true God,
begotten, not made,
of one being with the Father.

Through him all things were made.
For us and for our salvation
he came down from heaven:
by the power of the Holy Spirit
he became incarnate from the Virgin Mary,
and was made man.
For our sake he was crucified under Pontius Pilate;
he suffered death and was buried.
On the third day he rose again
in accordance with the Scriptures;
he ascended into heaven
and is seated at the right hand of the Father.
He will come again in glory
to judge the living and the dead,
and his kingdom will have no end.

We believe in the Holy Spirit, the Lord, the giver of life,
who proceeds from the Father [and the Son].
With the Father and the Son
he is worshipped and glorified.
He has spoken through the Prophets.

We believe in one holy catholic and apostolic Church.
We acknowledge one baptism for the forgiveness of sins.
We look for the resurrection of the dead,
and the life of the world to come. Amen.

The Lord Jesus Christ, as both truly man and truly God in his incarnation, meant that for the first time in the ancient world, a rational knowledge of God could be developed! God himself, present in Jesus Christ, could be rationally examined and cognitively understood. It is here that early Christianity stands strikingly apart from all previous pagan religions. Although Roman and Greek mythology had some surface similarities with the new, historically revealed Christian religion, Christianity and paganism stand here completely disparate in that humankind can now begin the rational science of knowing God himself in the humanity of the Lord Jesus Christ!

In his exceptionally well-documented and well-argued book, *The Victory of Reason*, Professor Rodney Stark, a social theorist, shows that in the cultures of China, Japan, Rome, and Greece, as well as in the religions of Islam and Judaism, a rational theology of God simply could not be formed.[61] Stark convincingly argues that a reasoned knowledge and theology of God did not appear anywhere in the world until Christian thinkers like the early church fathers, the second- and third-century apologists, and the medieval and Reformation theologians wrote and talked about God from the historical life and ministry of the God-man, Jesus Christ, as he is rationally known in the Scriptures. This knowledge of God led to the rational science of theology, an accomplishment rediscovered in our own day by Thomas F. Torrance in his epic book, *Theological Science*.[62]

Finally, the world had something to hold on to in the humanity of God in Jesus Christ! More and more elaborate and detailed theology could be written over the ages based on the words and deeds of the historical Jesus. This developing rational knowledge of God had huge ramifications, going far beyond the sphere of religion. Rational knowledge of God, as Stark observes, led to the rational discovery of the natural world by the natural sciences like physics, astronomy, and biology. Professor Stark writes:

> The Christian image of God is that of a rational being who *believes in human progress*, more fully revealing himself as humans *gain* the capacity to better understand. Moreover, because God is a rational being and the universe is his personal creation, it necessarily has a rational, lawful, stable structure, *awaiting increased human comprehension*. This was the key to many intellectual undertakings, among them the rise of science.[63]

The Bible stands or falls with the historical Jesus. And so does our search for almighty God. Hopefully, the reader will find that our case for the authentic words and deeds of Jesus, and for the testimony from New Testament witnesses, stands.

ONE SATURDAY NIGHT

The last chapter ended with the electricity of two influential people in my life: Mr. Cooper and his Bible study class and Mr. Clifton, a teacher at Richmond Hill High School. The dialectical debate of their opposite worldviews prompted in me an immense thirst for finding answers. Question after question, on every moral, philosophical, and theological issue, seemed to be raised with Mr. Cooper on Sunday afternoons as he led in our Bible study class. Mr. Clifton raised the bar high with discussions of vegetarianism, pacifism, communism, and classical books and music. However, there was much more than just learning information going on. Something else was happening on two levels in Reverend Cooper's class.

First, there was my fascination and satisfaction with how the Bible could answer every question I asked. It was such an inspiration to my mind and heart to hear reasonable, clear, and profound answers to my questions that I began to long to share these answers with as many of my generation as possible. I realized later in life that this was the beginning of not only my call to be a minister of the church, but to speak as widely as possible to my generation as an evangelist!

On another level, I was personally drawn to Jack Cooper and his highly spirited wife, Helen—to their humor, their compassion for me and their world, their hope and trust in God, their intellect in understanding their world and the Bible, and their unending capacity to enjoy a good time.

I wasn't sure which drew me more to God—their teaching or their personalities!

Then, in my last year of high school, Mr. Cooper asked the inevitable question of those of us who were seeking after God in a class like his: "I will be starting membership classes next week," he said, "and anyone who would like to receive Jesus Christ as their Lord and Savior and would like to demonstrate their faith by joining the church, please attend."

For some reason, despite having faith in God and a good knowledge of the church and Jesus Christ, I didn't feel ready to take the next step of a personal commitment to Christ and church membership. For the next week, I struggled with these thoughts. I didn't feel comfortable taking any new steps of faith.

Saturday came, and a stranger walked up the laneway to our home at Maple. He introduced himself to me as a Jehovah's Witness as we met outside the house. "Do you believe in God?" he asked. "Yes, I am certain there is a God," I answered. He continued to question where I stood on matters of faith. Little did he know that he was helping me sort through the spiritual turmoil of that week!

"I have been in a great class studying the Bible, and the teacher has asked us if we want to become Christians and join the local church," I told him. The visitor asked me about the beliefs of the Presbyterian Church and explained some things about what the Jehovah's Witnesses believe.

"What do you want to do with your life?" he asked me. "I really don't know," I answered. Then he gave me a challenge I really needed to hear, one that must have come from God himself. "Why don't you pray tonight until you get an answer from God about what he wants you to do with your life?" he proposed.

"Thank you very much. Definitely, I will pray tonight for God's will," I answered. I could see that this was a great way forward on these issues of commitment to Jesus Christ and church membership.

After supper, I went to my bedroom upstairs, opened my Bible, and asked God to speak to me just as he had to the prophets in the Old Testament. I wasn't looking for any emotional feelings about God's will. I wanted an audible voice from God from heaven above! After all, didn't God speak with many people in the Bible like that?

An hour went by of intense struggle with God in prayer. Nothing. Not even a still small voice in my bedroom!

I began to open my Bible and look to familiar places where I had found inspiration before. Another anxious hour passed, unlike the brief times of prayer before this night. In my frustration I said, "Lord, I think you are not going to speak to me in audible words or you would have done so already. Lord, I am going to open my Bible to wherever it falls open, and I ask you to speak to me from that passage. I know the Bible is called the Word of God, and I know you can speak to me from it."

I took my Bible, and it opened to the very last page in the entire book. My eyes fell upon the last invitation to come by faith to Jesus Christ in the entire Scripture:

And the Spirit and the bride [the church] say, Come.

And let him that heareth say, Come.

And let him that is athirst come.

And whosoever will, let him take the water of life freely. (Revelation 22:17, KJV)

In those words, God spoke to my mind and my heart! In my great thirst and longing for God, I came at that minute to the Lord Jesus Christ and asked for the gift of that water of life. I knew that Jesus was the Living Water, and I rejoiced as I asked him to come into my life and refresh me and be my Savior. At that moment, I became a Christian as I received Jesus Christ into my life. I wrote in the front of my Bible, "Born December 10 and reborn by the Spirit of God, June 9, 1963."

I enthusiastically went to church the next morning and told Mr. Cooper that I had accepted Christ and wanted to join the church! Within a few months after my confirmation, I acknowledged God's call upon my life to become a minister.

This became the starting point of a new life with God. Just as God had revealed himself to be the First Cause of everything and the Intelligent Designer of the creation that I had been born into as a human being, I now began a new creation in a personal relationship with this same God through the Lord Jesus Christ. I knew Jesus not just from his words, his miraculous deeds, and the testimonies to him in the Bible and from my teacher Jack Cooper, but in my own personal experience with God himself through Jesus Christ.

We have seen that God is evident in creation as the Intelligent Designer and First Cause. We have also seen, through the words and deeds of Jesus and the testimonies about him, that God entered history, incarnate in Jesus Christ. But is this all we need to know about Jesus? Does this fully explain *why* God came into the world? Does this answer everything we need to know about God?

The world Jesus was born into remained dead to God, "dead in sins and trespasses" (Ephesians 2:1), even as he ministered to it. We experience that emptiness and dissatisfaction in our own time from the endless seeking after brief pleasures to replace that deeper, lasting joy and satisfying life that we can only have when reconciled to God. And *that*, the Bible tells us, is the problem that the Son of God came into the world to solve!

That problem remained unconquered until the end of Jesus's life. The full remedy for humankind's spiritual sickness unto death happened next, at Jesus's crucifixion. This was where humanity's deepest problems with God were finally resolved. The crucifixion answers for us why Jesus came. Jesus called the ultimate solution to the problem of sin, "my hour to be glorified." It happened at the cross of Calvary.

CHAPTER 6
Jesus's Death:
A Tragic Martyr?

D oes the meaning and purpose shown in the life of the historical Jesus collapse at the point of his dying on a cruel cross? How could this tragic, apparently senseless, death have any merit for a positive understanding of Jesus of Nazareth? And what does Jesus's crucifixion mean to *our* search for God if Jesus, proclaimed as God with us, Immanuel, died an ignominious death?

Some skeptical scholars see Jesus's death as a great miscalculation that led to a meaningless and tragic end. They recognize that Jesus did ride into Jerusalem on Palm Sunday on a donkey, recognizing his attempt to fulfill a messianic prophecy in Zechariah 9:9 which reads:

> Rejoice greatly, O daughter Zion! Shout aloud, O daughter of Jerusalem! Lo, your king comes to you; triumphant and victorious is he, humble and riding on a donkey, on a colt, the foal of a donkey.

Liberal scholars, like New Testament professors Marcus Borg and John Dominic Crossan (of The Jesus Seminar), writing in their book, *The Last Week*,[64] admit they don't know why Jesus chose to enact such a risky fulfillment of prophecy at this precarious time, during a national holiday in Jerusalem. Furthermore, Crossan observes that Jesus put himself in great jeopardy when he cleansed the Temple of the sellers of sacrificial animals and the money changers in the sight of the Jewish officials there.

The American ABC television network did a special documentary, *Answering the Search for Jesus*, with host Peter Jennings,[65] that was highly critical of the New Testament. Just after the beginning of the show, they reported that there was "very little factual evidence for the historical Jesus," and it went steadily downhill after that. Several Jesus Seminar fringe scholars, like Robert Funk, Marcus Borg, John Crossan, and Marvin Meyer, were featured throughout the documentary, saying that things began to get entirely out of hand on that day before Good Friday in Jerusalem. These religious thinkers believe that the Jewish authorities never intended Jesus's death, but when they turned Jesus over to the Roman procurator, Pontius Pilate, things went completely crazy. Without the Jews' intending it, Jesus was not only beaten severely, but was sentenced to death on a cross and executed.

Thus, some of these thinkers conclude that Jesus died a martyr's meaningless and senseless death because of his own bad judgment regarding the volatile and unstable conditions in Jerusalem at the time of the Jewish feast of the Passover. There's a lot at stake here if this observation is true: how can Jesus reveal God to us if his life ended with such a human miscalculation and tragic failure?

Even some clergy today seem to be embarrassed by the death of Jesus, shunning the powerful "blood hymns" of previous generations in the church. One of these was a famous New York minister, Harry Emerson Fosdick, who wrote many popular books, including one especially helpful book called *The Meaning of Prayer*,[66] a guide to personal prayer enjoyed by many branches of the Christian church. But Fosdick could make no sense of the bloody death of Jesus on his cross, comparing some references to his death in the Bible to the ancient practices of pagan priests to satisfy their gods by animal sacrifices: "Must we, then, go on forever, using the analogy of bloody animal sacrifice to express our interpretation of Christ's death? I answer emphatically, No!"[67] Fosdick remained unable to appreciate the power of the blood of Christ shed at the cross, the undeniable evidence of a life taken on our behalf.

Prior to the crucifixion, even Jesus's chief apostle, Peter, refused to accept any idea of Jesus dying in Jerusalem on a cross. In Caesarea Philippi, when Peter confessed his faith in Jesus as Messiah, the Son of God, Jesus saw the need to prepare his disciples for his coming death in Jerusalem under the authorities. This mission to die seemed completely incredible to Peter, who took the Lord aside and "rebuked him, saying, 'God forbid it, Lord! This must never happen to you'" (Matthew 16:22).

There is something very human and understandable in Peter's refusal to accept Jesus's tragic coming death. That is the way the human mind works in this world—just like Peter, many of us think that the good should be blessed and the wicked suffer! Such a tragic death must never happen to the Lord.

Yet Jesus knew this was why he had come into the world. Matthew writes,

> But the Lord turned and said to Peter, "Get behind me Satan! You are a stumbling block to me; for you are setting your mind not on divine things but on human things." (Matthew 16:23)

It seems that Jesus was the only one who *didn't* see death as a problem to his claims to being God. But what sense can we ever make of Jesus's horrible crucifixion on a wooden cross?

TURNING DEATH INTO DESTINY

Paradoxically, what may appear to be the weakest and most incomprehensible part of the story of Jesus Christ has become the strongest and most powerful part of the good news proclaimed by his disciples, with implications for all people and all religions of the world. The crucifixion of Jesus began a complete revolution in the destiny of all humankind in every region, culture, and religion of the world—a revolution dated from exactly three o'clock on a datable afternoon on that first Good Friday in history! What happened?

Jesus's death was so significant that almost one third of the Gospel of Mark, and almost half of the Gospel of John, dwells on the last week of his life. The foremost thinker among the apostles, Paul, spent almost his entire life as a Christian writing, reflecting, and preaching almost exclusively on *two days* in the life of Jesus—what we now call Good Friday (Jesus's death) and Easter Sunday (Jesus's resurrection).

Paul, as we read in the Acts of the Apostles, was a brilliant and courageous preacher who wrote letters filled with deep theological ideas. Yet what captivated Paul over and over again in his epistles was the crucifixion and resurrection of Jesus Christ. Here Paul begins his first letter to the intellectual believers in Corinth:

> When I came to you, brothers and sisters, I did not come proclaiming the mystery of God in lofty words or wisdom. For I decided to know nothing among you except Jesus Christ, and him crucified. (1 Corinthians 2:1–2)

Paul repeats this testimony to the death and resurrection of the Lord over and over again. Writing to his beloved believers in Philippi, Paul testifies,

> Yet whatever gains I had, these I have come to regard as loss because of Christ . . . I want to know Christ and the power of his resurrection and the sharing of his sufferings by becoming like him in his death, if somehow I may attain the resurrection from the dead. (Philippians 3:7, 10)

While some Christian churches today try to avoid emphasizing the "blood of Calvary," the New Testament makes the shedding of Jesus's blood its strongest argument in presenting its message to the world. The crucifixion of Jesus was not popular even then with their fellow Jews or the sophisticated Greeks! To the Jews, Christ's death was scandalous and humiliating—that the Messiah should suffer and die was unthinkable, and the Jews had a particular revulsion for death by crucifixion because of Old Testament laws that proclaimed "cursed is everyone who is hung on a tree" (Galatians 3:13, NIV). The intellectual and philosophical Greeks, on the other hand, thought this message of Jesus's death was complete nonsense and foolishness. If the Christians proclaimed Jesus as God, how could this man die? the Greeks might ask. However, Paul presents Jesus's death as the greatest part of his message:

> For Jews demand signs and Greeks desire wisdom, but we proclaim Christ crucified a stumbling block to Jews and foolishness to Gentiles, but to those who are called, both Jews and Greeks, Christ the power of God and the wisdom of God. For God's foolishness is wiser than human wisdom, and God's weakness is stronger than human strength. (1 Corinthians 1:22–25)

Many people in North America view Jesus as a great teacher who came "to preach the good news of the Fatherhood of God and the brotherhood of man," as summarized by nineteenth-century German historian Adolf Harnack, in his epoch-making book, *What Is Christianity?*[68] But is that truly the heart of Christianity? How does Jesus's death on a cross answer our original, crucial question about finding information and faith in the living God? Why, according to Jesus himself, did Jesus come? And how does his death fit our quest for God?

Did Jesus ever tell us why he came to earth? And is his explanation of why he died reliable?

JESUS SETS OFF A REVOLUTION

In fact, Jesus *did* tell us why he came many times in the four Gospel histories. For example, all these Gospels give the same account of

Jesus praying in the garden of Gethsemane on the night in which he was betrayed. In this harrowing scene, Jesus agonizes over his coming death with drops of sweat like blood from his mental torment over what he felt was the Father's will for him. If there was any other way to fulfill his earthly purpose, he prayed, then "let this cup pass from me" (Matthew 26:39). But Jesus steadfastly followed the Father's plan of salvation set out in the Jewish Scriptures.

In those Scriptures we learn that, from the very first man and woman in history, God's plan was for the offspring of this woman to destroy the agent, Satan, who brought temptation, sin, and consequently death to our first parents and to all their succeeding generations. This plan is foreshadowed and prophesied throughout the Old Testament. Yet, except for Jesus, no one in the New Testament had the foresight to see how God was *now* accomplishing this plan of salvation for humanity.

The gospel emphasis is clear: it was this night of sweating blood in the garden and the next day of his death for which Jesus had come to earth—not just to teach and call his disciples to found a church or start a new religion. Jesus had come from the Father primarily to die on the cross.

The clearest place we see Jesus's purpose and mission for his death is in the Gospel of John, where Jesus refuses to be recognized as Messiah until his "time had come" (John 2:4; John 7:6; John 12:27 ff; see also Matthew 26:18).

One of the signals to Jesus that his time *had* come occurred near the end of his ministry in Jerusalem, when some Greeks in the holy city, themselves proselytes of the Jewish religion, came to the apostle Philip and asked him, "Sir, we wish to see Jesus" (John 12: 21). The Lord saw that his ministry to the Jews was complete and that now the Gentile world was coming to him as well. When Jesus met the Greeks, he proclaimed to the crowd gathered there exactly why he had come:

"The hour has come for the Son of Man to be glorified . . . Now my soul is troubled. And what should I say— 'Father, save me from this hour'? No, it is for this reason

that I have come to this hour . . . Now is the judgment
of this world; now the ruler of this world will be driven
out. And I, when I am lifted up from the earth, will draw
all people to myself." He said this to indicate the kind of
death he was to die (John 12:23, 27, 31–32).

The second-to-last sentence in this quotation is rich with meaning: "And I, when I am lifted up from the earth, will draw all people to myself." Here we see three significant aspects of Jesus's mission: Jesus's *egotism*, Jesus's *magnetism*, and Jesus's *optimism*.

Already we have seen the egotism of our Lord, revealed in his being both the Law and Lawgiver in the Sermon on the Mount. In the above verse, Jesus speaks of himself in the first person three times: "I," "I," "myself." The Lord offers himself to the world as its Savior. Jesus did not point away from himself to someone else, solely to God the Father, as did all the other prophets, priests, kings, and disciples in the Bible—and as all the prophets and founders of other world religions also do.

Rather, he offered himself, the Savior of humanity, and claimed that it would be through his death on the cross that he would achieve this salvation. The egotism of Jesus, found again here in John's gospel, calls us to worship him!

What magnetism Jesus's cross has for the whole world! The cross displays the power of God's love just like the self-sacrificing love of a mother for her children. Wounded and hurting people in every age, with lives broken by sin and tragedy, somehow recognize in the cross of Jesus Christ the power and magnetism of God to draw them to himself. At the cross, God is not distant, far away, and indifferent to us, but he feels our pain and loves us before we are even ready to be loved. The message of the cross has a power we can actually feel! It is the exact opposite of a terrible tragedy that humankind must turn its eyes away from.

So what exactly is it about the cross that magnetically drew Paul and the other disciples to Jesus? At first, almost all his followers fled and hid themselves from Golgotha where Jesus was crucified. That may be our first reaction too. But when the apostles reviewed the Jewish Scriptures after Jesus's resurrection, they were magnetically drawn to his death. The reason for this attraction to the cross can be found in the last words Jesus spoke there. These three words, when his disciples looked back later, summarized everything the Lord had come to do. These last three words, spoken with his dying breath and recorded in John 19:30, were:

"It is finished."

WORDS OF GLORIOUS HOPE

Jesus's last words could have the obvious meaning that his terrible pain and agony, caused by the nails through his hands and feet, had finally come to an end as he died. Or they could mean that Jesus's ministry as teacher and lord had come to an end. However, in the context of many of Jesus's teachings and of the Old Testament prophecies concerning the coming Messiah, there is another, far greater meaning to "it is finished." It is this meaning that ultimately gave rise to the Christian faith.

Jesus anticipated his death from the beginning and taught that this moment was his mission in life. "It is finished!" is a divine cry, proclaiming that the old order of the world had come to an end as he breathed his last breath. Just what is this old regime that is finished and has come to an end?

Jesus's words reveal that *the work of world religions is finished*. The religions of the world had long labored to make people good enough to go to heaven, but they had never triumphed in this. That order had now been cast down and destroyed by the free gift of grace through the cross.

All religions offer moral laws and principles to follow that will improve the moral and spiritual lives of their followers. One can think of the Law of Moses in the Old Testament, the Koran of the Muslims, or the Hindu and Buddhist Scriptures, all filled with good ethical teachings to make their followers into better and better people. And these laws do contribute to a better world. But the final judgment by God is menaced by the inadequacy of all human good works and the moral observances that have not been fully kept.

It may be a truism for all religions that the righteous will be rewarded and the wicked will be punished, despite the fact that some religions also factor in references to the grace of a merciful God. But the common standard for everyone, whether karma in eastern religions or the final judgment of God for others, is the disturbing uncertainty of a good outcome!

The grace of the cross does not deny that God wants people to be morally good. Nevertheless, the greatest and most righteous spiritual leaders, those who are closest to God, admit to sin in their lives, demonstrating that none of us can ever fulfill all God's laws and thus be certain of his or her place in heaven. (The one exception to this is Jesus Christ himself, whom the Bible teaches was without sin. Muslims also believe and teach this about Christ.)

Although the Hebrew Scriptures offer many moral laws and precepts, they are fully cognizant of this problem. King David, inspired by God, wrote of God's universal indictment and verdict against humanity:

> They have all turned aside; together they have become corrupt; there is none who does good, not even one. (Psalm 14:3, ESV)

In the New Testament, Paul, the former Pharisee, gives the same verdict from God as King David did:

> All have sinned and fall short of the glory of God. (Romans 3:23)

Sometimes humanity tires of religion. We cannot always live up to our own standards, whatever they are or wherever they come from. It's frustrating to be told what to do when we cannot consistently and flawlessly do it. It fact, it seems that the most religious people, the ones who hunger and thirst most for righteousness, feel themselves to be the greatest moral failures. It certainly was that way with St. Paul, a paragon of faith and morals amongst his peers who desperately felt a moral wreck in life:

> For we know that the law is spiritual; but I am of the flesh, sold into slavery under sin. I do not understand my own actions. For I do not do what I want, but I do the very thing I hate . . . For I delight in the law of God in my inmost self, but I see in my members another law at war with the law of my mind, making me captive to the law of sin that dwells in my members. Wretched man that I am! Who will rescue me from this body of death? Thanks be to God through Jesus Christ our Lord! (Romans 7:14–15, 22–25)

Paul and King David are the story of every person. We cannot be good enough to be certain of earning a place in heaven. The harder we try, the greater our sense of failure. This experience of moral shortcoming is universal—a law as consistent and telling as the natural laws that surround us.

How can humankind search for and find God when we are so tainted in our search by sin? How can we know and respond to the God of nature when the verdict from the God of the Bible convicts everyone of the inadequacy of our best efforts to find him?

Here is the answer: Jesus not only reveals this hidden God of nature but brings with him the solution to the all-too-human problem of sin. And he does this at the point of his death.

We need a different paradigm than good works: a new plan, a revolution from the judgments of religion. And that, according to Jesus's own claims and the testimony of his followers, is why Jesus came! He came to live a perfect life without sin in our place, to clothe us with his righteousness which we receive by faith in him. What we will never be good enough to earn by religious observance, God now freely gives us at the cross of Christ. Christ lived in our place the life we ought to live and died in our place the death we deserve for our sins. We receive this gift of forgiveness and eternal life only at the cross of Jesus Christ and only as a pure gift, something we could never earn! Paul sums it up best:

> For by grace you have been saved through faith, and this is not your own doing; it is the gift of God—not a result of works, so that no one may boast. (Ephesians 2:8–9)

This is what is meant by the term *gospel*—literally, "good news." This is the heart of Christianity and the crux of God's coming into our history to act in our lives. This all happened when Jesus said "it is finished." The old era of works has ended, and the revolution of salvation by grace has begun! What a good day! What a Good Friday! In fact, this is the *only* truly good day in the history of the world!

What about God's requirements in the law for good works? Paul says immediately following Ephesians 2:8–9 above that God has made us for the very purpose of doing good works, although we can never earn our salvation from them:

> For we are His workmanship, created in Christ Jesus for good works, which God prepared beforehand, that we should walk in them. (Ephesians 2:10, ESV)

The Bible teaches that our good works can never add to the grace God has freely given us at the cross. When we receive all of God's gifts, we are able to respond to God with our faithful and obedient works in answer to his love. The apostle John gives an insight into our response to God's mercy at the cross:

> Beloved, let us love one another, because love is from God; everyone who loves is born of God and knows God. Whoever does not love does not know God, for God is love . . . In this is love, *not that we loved God, but that He loved us* and sent His Son to be the atoning sacrifice for our sins. (1 John 4:7–8, 10)

Thus Jesus not only reveals the true God, but reconciles us, as an estranged humanity, to himself. It comes by way of a gift. One of the best ways of being certain that we have received God's free gift of salvation is through the assurance of God's words given to us in Scripture and the love we express to God and others in obedience to God's amazing, free grace!

Finally, notice the optimism of the Lord in John 12:32: "And I, when I am lifted up from the earth, will draw all people to myself." This good news of the gospel will exclude no one. It is for everyone seeking God and assurance of eternal life! Jesus had the optimism that, when he was lifted up on the cross, all of the world would be drawn to him.

This, then, is the message that every sincere seeker after God must hear and grapple with. Scripture teaches that God did for us what we were never able to do for ourselves. Jesus was the second Person of God, the Son, coming to reveal the Father and his love. And Jesus died on the cross to end the era of the judgment of the world's religions by giving the world a gift they could never achieve on their own.

There is a famous sentence in John's gospel, a summary statement of all that Jesus came to reveal and to do for us:

> For God so loved the world that He gave His *one and only Son, that whoever believes* in Him shall not perish but have *eternal life.* (John 3:16, NIV, emphasis mine)

IN DESPERATE NEED OF FORGIVENESS

After graduating from high school, followed by a BA from the University of Toronto, I began a three-year honors BD program at New College, University of Edinburgh, in Scotland. I went to Edinburgh to pursue knowledge of almighty God. Up until that time, I had lived a fairly moral, upright life. There had been some bumps in my youthful behavior that I felt ashamed about, but like many "good" people today, I felt that I was a fairly honorable young man. This perception of myself as a fairly good person did not change much when I became a Christian. I accepted Jesus because I believed in him as God, and although convinced of my own sin, I still thought I was not a totally bad person.

Thus, when we said the confession of sins in church, it meant very little to me. Yes, I knew there was pride in my life, jealousy, and of course, lust. However, I felt little guilt. I knew that by comparison to some of my friends at university, I was a fairly good person.

Then there came an incident as a twenty-three-year-old Canadian living in Edinburgh that destroyed my perennial sense of moral decency. Of all the times of the year, it was Easter Weekend, when many of the local theological students had gone home for Holy Week. It was the end of my second year there, and I was very lonely on the Saturday night between Good Friday and Easter Sunday. One of my friends told me there was going to be a party for the international students at a hall behind our residence. I thought maybe this would offer company for me at a very lonely time on a spiritually draining day in the Christian calendar.

There were several hundred students there from all over Europe and overseas, a lot of noise, and a great deal of wine flowing. Standing beside two women from Ireland, I began a conversation that soon drew in another man, a little older than the three of us. Later we learned that he was an announcer on the major local radio station. The talk and the wine continued to flow.

The party ended early out of respect for the day, and the older man in our group invited the three of us to his favorite restaurant across the city. He drove us there in his car. After the champagne ran out, he ordered his choice of wine, called Bull's Blood. I was tired and had very little sense, and I got quite drunk on this important night for Christians.

Near dawn, the radio announcer invited us to travel with him out of the city to another restaurant to have breakfast. The morning dragged on and on and on. I saw people going to church as we traveled in the car. And for the first time in so many years that I couldn't remember it ever happening before, I completely missed going to church on Easter Sunday morning. When I finally got back to the New College residence, it was about noon, Sunday, and I was overwhelmed with guilt.

My behavior that day may not sound too shocking to the reader, but for me, it was eyeopening. I finally saw my true condition. I had gotten drunk on a high Christian holiday, had been a terrible example to the others in our group, and hadn't even been to church to share in the greatest hope of the world, to celebrate Jesus's resurrection! What a mess I had suddenly become! What a spiritual wreck I was!

That evening, I was one of the first to show up at a historic church close by the university residence, called the Church of the Greyfriers. I felt so ashamed and unworthy to be in church that night—until the minister led us all in a prayer of confession. Many of the things we said in that prayer seemed to pertain to me specifically, and I felt the guilt falling from my shoulders with each word as we confessed our sins together as a congregation.

At the end of the prayer of confession, the minister said a verse called "the Assurance of Pardon," to assure the penitent that they are now forgiven by God:

> If we confess our sins, he who is faithful and just will forgive us our sins and cleanse us from all unrighteousness. (1 John 1:9)

How welcome those words were! Never before in my life had I possessed such a sense of my need for forgiveness. To confess my sins before God and be assured of his forgiveness was tremendously cleansing and uplifting. I started to feel restored in my relationship with God. I could start to forgive myself and not blame the three others for going so wrong the night before.

And that is a large part of why Jesus came into the world. Despite many people thinking they are basically good people, doing the best they can, and having little sense of their need of forgiveness, there come times in so many lives when our souls are hurting and crushed by our tragic mistakes and sins. It is the testimony of the Bible and of history that God, our loving heavenly Father, cares about us enough to restore us and lift us up again.

Jesus did all this for us. Jesus shows us the humanity of God and helps us to see and touch the Divine. But he also lived a completely righteous life in our place to clothe us with his righteousness and died in our place to pay the penalty for our sins. When we receive his forgiveness at the cross, his grace and the gift of eternal life, we can be assured of pardon and never fear being rejected again.

As I did in the night service at the Greyfriers Church in Edinburgh, everyone can find from this same God forgiveness and help to continue on. That is why Jesus came. That constitutes the heart of the good news of the gospel of Jesus Christ! That is the message that the hidden God of creation wants us to know.

Forgiveness is foundational for finding and knowing the living God, and Jesus enables us to find it. Without the forgiveness of our sins, we can never stand in the proper place for a true relationship with a holy God. Jesus not only reveals God to the world, but reconciles us to God so we can have a meaningful relationship with the Holy One.

Christian churches around the world celebrate Good Friday during Holy Week each year. It is a solemn day to remember and observe the intense suffering of our Lord for the lost world he came to save. But in our hearts and our minds on Good Friday, we strain forward, knowing already how this will all turn out. Good Friday forgives us, and Easter Sunday completes the mission of Christ. We look to that Easter Sunday morning next.

CHAPTER 7
Resurrection

T he most important conversion of any man in the entire history of the Christian church happened on a Roman road threading its way from Jerusalem northward to Damascus, Syria. It was only several years after the crucifixion of Jesus of Nazareth, and this man had a deep hatred for the growing group of people, mainly Jews, who still held allegiance to the dead teacher from Galilee, Jesus.

This hostile man's name was Saul, and he sought out followers of "the Way," these followers of Jesus, to imprison them and possibly execute them for what he considered blasphemy against God and the traditions of the elders of his people. Saul was a man with much contempt and bitterness in his heart.

However, as much as he was violently repelled by these followers of Jesus, he was also, in a maddening way, attracted to their love and their peacefulness in the face of terrible persecution. He must have wondered at different points of contact, "What makes these deplorable people so faithful to this mystifying man from Galilee? What is their secret?"

Saul's self-doubt in his mission paradoxically made him all the more resolute in his attack on the Christians.

Acts 9 tells us that Saul was in pursuit of these believers all the way to Syria in the company of several others when a blinding light made him fall to the ground. Then he heard a voice—his companions said it sounded like thunder, but Saul could hear the words of an audible voice from heaven saying, "Saul, Saul, why do you persecute me?"

Saul had terrible hatred in his heart, but he was also, in a strange way, a godly man—a man who had to know the truth no matter what the consequences would be.

Saul summoned all his courage and dared to experiment with this voice from above: "Who are you, Lord?" Saul wanted to know the truth—had this voice something to do with his mission, his career, his future destiny? Fear of God gripped his heart when he heard the reply: "I am Jesus whom you are persecuting" (Acts 9:1–9). Utter dismay fell upon this ruined man. What could this possibly mean?

Often, harsh antagonists who come to Christ from other religions or from great embitterment toward God seem to require a series of unusual and clearly providential events to turn their lives from hatred and contempt to humble submission and love toward Jesus Christ. The Bible calls such events "signs and wonders" that accompany God's work of conversion in a lost man's heart.

It was certainly true for Saul. He was struck to the ground and blinded by this bolt of light, physically and spiritually shaken as he had to be led by his companions to Damascus.

At the same time, another miraculous event was taking place in Damascus: a believer by the name of Ananias was having a vision from God telling him to go and meet with Saul. Here is the Bible account of it:

> But Ananias answered, "Lord, I have heard from many about this man, how much evil he has done to your saints in Jerusalem; and here he has authority from the chief priests to bind all who invoke your name." But the Lord said to him, "Go, for he is an instrument whom I

have chosen to bring my name before Gentiles and kings and before the people of Israel" . . .

So Ananias went and entered the house. He laid his hands on Saul and said, "Brother Saul, the Lord Jesus, who appeared to you on your way here, has sent me so that you may regain your sight and be filled with the Holy Spirit." And immediately something like scales fell from his eyes, and his sight was restored. Then he got up and was baptized, and after taking some food, he regained his strength. (Acts 9:13–19)

It took all these extraordinary sign and wonders to convert Saul, now known as Paul, to become a man God could greatly use. And how magnificently Paul was used! Paul entered the history of the church at an extremely critical point, helping to lay with others in the apostolic community the foundations for the entire Christian faith, "with Jesus Christ himself the cornerstone" (Ephesians 2:20). And now, just like the other apostles, Paul was also a witness of the resurrected Lord Jesus Christ, and consequently qualified to become an apostle of the Lord Jesus himself.

Paul may never have had the opportunity to hear Jesus teach in Galilee or see his miracles throughout the region of Judea, but like all the other apostles, Paul was a witness of the bodily resurrected Lord Jesus Christ!

This is the climax of our presentation of Jesus Christ, or rather, of God visible in human history in Jesus. Jesus of Nazareth may have been born truly God and truly man, he may have come to make payment for our sins, but all this is largely meaningless if his bones are still decaying in the earth today, still harbored in the borrowed tomb his body entered on Good Friday.

If our search for God has led us to creation, then to the historical Jesus, and then to the cross, it must lead us beyond these things as well—it must lead us to resurrection.

PAUL: A KNOWN LIAR OR TELLING THE TRUTH?

Paul knew what a deliberate lie his letters in the New Testament would be before both God and men if he proclaimed the resurrection without being a witness himself to the resurrected Lord and meeting other eyewitnesses who had also met the bodily resurrected Lord. The apostles stood in a gifted place in history as witnesses of the resurrected Lord.

For believers today, Jesus said, "Blessed are those who have not seen, and yet have come to believe" (John 20:29). The whole Christian faith today rests on the eyewitnesses in the Scripture and our own unseen personal experiences of the risen Lord Jesus. Paul makes it clear in no uncertain terms to the new believers in the Greek city of Corinth, where he had started a church, that Jesus Christ rose from the dead:

> Now if Christ is proclaimed as raised from the dead, how can some of you say there is no resurrection of the dead? If there is no resurrection of the dead, then Christ has not been raised; and if Christ has not been raised, then our proclamation has been in vain and your faith has been in vain. We are even found to be misrepresenting God, because we testified of God that he raised Christ . . . If for this life only we have hoped in Christ, we are of all people most to be pitied. (1 Corinthians 15:12–19)

THE GREATEST EVENT FROM THE BEGINNING

Often, critics of the resurrection suggest that belief in this event didn't develop until much later, maybe one or two hundred years after the ministry of Jesus, and was the invention of what was then emerging as the Roman Catholic Church.[69] However, many scholars, as evidenced in the *English Standard Version Study Bible*,[70] see in 1 Corinthians 15:3–9 the very first official statement and creed in Christian history, and the resurrection is central to it! Once again, it is Paul who offers us a unique glimpse into how the resurrection of Jesus Christ impacted the church within the first two dozen years after the empty tomb. This creed, written about 55 AD—about twenty years following the resurrection—is a summary of early Christian belief that probably dates originally from months after the resurrection itself.

Even though some religious writers deny that Jesus ever lived, they do admit that Paul appeared at this time in history. In his book *The Pagan Christ*,[71] former New Testament professor Tom Harpur accepts that Paul's letters have very distinct themes, precisely expressed, which are truly distinct to Paul. In this letter to the church at Corinth, Paul is very autobiographical, making frequent allusions to himself and his circumstances. This letter then can clearly be stated as coming from a first-century Jewish Christian by the name of Paul, writing to Christians in the Greek city of Corinth.[72]

Corinth had many problems as a city. It had over one million people, the second largest population outside of Rome, and was rife with pagan worship and moral corruption. Coming down from their temple shrines on the hills, temple prostitutes would offer themselves to devotees in Corinth. The temple of Apollo can still be seen there, and the ruins of the ancient main street remain to this day, with the foundations of shops and even public lavatories with toilet seats carved in stone. Corinth was also a trading center for merchants, with many sailors seeking the services of prostitutes and many other visitors seeking to satisfy their vices. The dictionary tells us that to *corinthicize* means to give oneself to wild living.

The believers in Corinth came into a Christian faith that was being newly established. Within fifty days of the resurrection, at Pentecost, new believers were added to the tiny community of disciples. Over the next weeks, months, and years, down to Paul's letter in 55 AD, as many new believers came into the church they were baptized, taught the gospel of the Lord, and allowed to partake with the church in the "breaking of bread" at Holy Communion.

Right from these very first months after the resurrection, the church would have a need for a brief summary of faith—a creed—for the new believers to recite at baptism and before partaking of bread at the Lord's Table. What is recorded in Paul's letter is just such an early essential statement of faith: scholars feel it was the first Christian creed for significant occasions. Here it is:

> For I handed on to you as of first importance what I in turn had received: that Christ died for our sins in accordance with the scriptures, and that he was buried, and that he was raised on the third day in accordance with the scriptures, and that he appeared to Cephas, then to the twelve. Then he appeared to more than five hundred brothers and sisters at one time, most of whom are still alive, though some have died. Then he appeared to James, then to all the apostles. Last of all, as to one untimely born, he appeared also to me. (1 Corinthians 15:3–8)

Here is a virtual window looking right into the history of the church in the first half of the first century! More than the Master's authoritative teachings, which at this time were being recorded in the Gospels, and more important than the recitation of Jesus's great miracles, *it was the resurrection of their crucified Lord that was the essence of the first Christian creed and the crucial statement of their most cherished belief!* Belief in the resurrection was not something added on to the historical Jesus later in history. Not only was it there from the beginning, but the resurrection was the church's most precious belief from the beginning. The gospel stands or falls on this historical event. The resurrection expands greatly our knowledge of creation's God and God's purposes for all humanity as we face our fragile mortality.

For Paul and others in the apostolic community, the death and resurrection of Jesus Christ formed the content of far more of their preaching and writing than anything else. This belief in the resurrection is so central to the entire message of the New Testament that references to it appear in almost every single book of the New Testament. From the earliest books written to the last, the resurrection is "of first importance," as it says in the resurrection creed recited by Paul.

TWO LAWYERS: FROM SKEPTICISM TO FAITH

Where does our original search for God at the beginning of this book now lead us? Where do we start to examine this belief? Is Jesus's so-called resurrection relevant to our knowledge of God? How do we discover if it is credible, and do we have enough evidence to believe in Jesus rising from the dead for ourselves today?

To check out the credibility of the resurrection, the place to start is by studying the references to it in the four gospel histories of Matthew 28, Mark 16, Luke 24, and John 20–21, as well as the significant passages in Acts 1, Romans 6, and 1 Corinthians 15. (It is a fascinating study to examine the sequence of appearances of the resurrected Lord in the Bible and see how each author has his own unique portrait from eyewitnesses—much like how the different viewpoints of competing media sources present the events of the primaries leading up to the election of an American president!)

Study of the details of the resurrection brings conviction of the truth of this event. In fact, some of the greatest books on the resurrection have come from unbelievers trying vigorously to disprove it by studying these biblical accounts! Rather than analyzing the biblical accounts here (I hope you will do that on your own), we will look at two skeptical authors who looked all the evidence over and came to the only reasonable conclusion about the resurrection: it is true.

An English lawyer by the name of Frank Morison had a reverent esteem for Jesus, although because of his study of early twentieth-century science, he had no faith in the miracles in the Gospels. Mr. Morison had a longing to restore some dignity to the life of Jesus without resorting to any claims of the miraculous. So he chose to examine the last seven days of Jesus's life. He gives his reasons for focusing on this brief final span:

1. This period seemed remarkably free from the miraculous element which on scientific grounds I held suspect.

2. All the Gospel writers devoted much space to this period, and, in the main, were strikingly in agreement.

3. The trial and execution of Jesus was a reverberating historical event, attested indirectly by a thousand political consequences and by a vast literature which grew out of them.[73]

This was the clean, antiseptic kind of portrait of Jesus that Morison wanted to write. He states his goal:

I wanted to take this Last Phase of the life of Jesus,
with all its quick and pulsating drama, its sharp, clear-cut
background of antiquity, and its tremendous psychological and human interest—to strip it of its overgrowth of
primitive beliefs and dogmatic suppositions, and to see
this supremely great Person as He really was.[74]

Morison poured all his energy into this study—and the ground
under him began to shake! Using his careful, analytical lawyer's
mind, he studied the details of these seven days in the Bible, along
with the even more crucial three days *after* the crucifixion, reading
much of the later literature relevant to his project. As he did, a different book than the one he had intended to write began to take
shape. Morison became a different man with an entirely different
book and a new faith in Jesus's bodily resurrection from the dead.

The result: a bestselling classic called *Who Moved The Stone?* On
the title page, under his name, Morison quoted the Apostles' Creed:
"Suffered under Pontius Pilate, was crucified, dead and buried . . .
The third day he rose again from the dead." As a result of his intense
research, Morison couldn't escape the logical and most compelling
conclusion—that Jesus died on the cross on Good Friday and rose
from the dead on Easter Sunday.

Even a man of immense intellect like Frank Morison, when
open to God and the claims of the Scriptures, will come to faith in
the resurrection of Jesus Christ.

AN INVESTIGATIVE REPORTER

This conversion story happened all over again, but this time in
Chicago, Illinois. Again, the skeptic was a lawyer, Lee Strobel, a

graduate from Yale Law School who worked as the legal editor of *The Chicago Tribune* until 1981. Lee couldn't believe that there even was any God at all. He writes of his life in 1981:

> To me—an atheist at the time—this [a completely inaccurate news story he had received from a distraught father about his daughter] was an apt analogy for the mindset of Christians. From my perspective, their faith blinded them to the real facts about Jesus, and they only saw what they wanted to see in him. Certainly he was only a legend or a mere mortal at best. In their wide-eyed gullibility, Christians sincerely believed he rose from the dead and thus proved he was the Son of God. But there was no doubt in my mind that they were sincerely wrong.[75]

Lee, at the time, enjoyed all the freedoms of an atheist with few moral restraints, but he loved his wife. When she came home one day and announced to Lee that she had become a Christian, Lee called this "the unthinkable." It was somewhat troubling to see "winsome changes in her character and values, which she attributed to God" over the following months. Now Lee became committed to studying Christianity so that, as he writes, "maybe I could liberate her from this cult."[76]

Lee Strobel used his legal acumen and journalistic investigative reporting to read the Bible accounts, to research the related literature, and even to travel to consult with the major spokesmen who had debated this belief on both sides. He broke down his investigation into three parts:

1. The Medical Evidence: Was Jesus' Death a Sham and His Resurrection a Hoax?
2. The Evidence of the Missing Body: Was Jesus' Body Really Absent from His Tomb?
3. The Evidence of Appearances: Was Jesus Seen Alive After His Death on the Cross?[77]

Lee sincerely wanted to dissuade his wife from a naive faith by destroying what he thought was the "linchpin of the Christian faith,"[78] the so-called miracle of the resurrection.

Slowly, as all the evidence came in, the verdict came in clear and true for Lee—innocent. The Bible tells the truth—Jesus rose bodily from the dead!

Lee's book is a hardheaded argument from a man with a sound mind and should be read by anyone wanting to know *The Case for Easter* for themselves.

Despite the evidence, some of the critics of the resurrection in St. Paul's day—such as the political, philosophical and aristocratic elites listening to Paul's sermon in Athens[79]—found his remarks on the resurrection too hard to believe. Many people today, possibly like the Athenians, find they can believe in the Creator, but stumble over the belief that Jesus could rise from the dead.

What problem do we have with believing this miracle of the crucified Jesus rising from the dead, if the biblical accounts have credibility? Is this feat too difficult for God? If God, the Creator of the cosmos and the omnipotent power behind the creation of everything, visited us and unveiled his glory in his Son Jesus Christ, is there really any question of this miracle being too hard for God?

One of the first popular translations of the New Testament in the 1960s came from biblical scholar J.B. Phillips, who wrote a companion book called *The Ring of Truth*.[80] When someone with an open mind and seeking heart reads the Bible, he observed, it creates the ringing impression of being the truth.

J.B. Phillips then went on to write another popular book called *Your God Is Too Small*.[81] The God revealed in the Bible is great enough to raise his Son from the dead! If you can't believe this well-documented miracle, your God is too small. Lawyer Lee Strobel couldn't believe anyone would find the resurrection credible but saw it was the centerpiece of the New Testament. Prove this miracle to be fatuous, and the case for Christianity, and probably for a personal God altogether, falls apart. But is there really a problem if the preceding arguments for God possessing omnipotent power as the creating First Cause and unlimited mind as the Intelligent Designer are true? Is raising Jesus from the dead too small or too hard a thing for God to do?

The resurrection of Jesus goes far beyond simply being a belief among some Christians; it has huge ramifications for finding any ultimate meaning in Jesus's ministry—and for the survival of all humankind from death itself!

Finding Out for Yourself

The time has come for you to find out for yourself the truth of what you have seen in this book. It is time for the great experiment.

When I took part in doctoral classes, we invited Archbishop Ted Scott, who was then the Primate of the Anglican Church in Canada, to attend. We doctoral students had many weighty questions for him to answer. He listened carefully to each question and then gave a thoughtful and often satisfying answer.

But at the end of the morning, after we had thanked him for coming and sharing so deeply with us, he said that at one time, when he had just graduated from divinity school, he had thought he had to have an answer for every question that people would ask him. But now he realized that it is much more adequate to simply point people to the resources of the Christian faith and let them work out the answers for themselves.

Those resources are still available.

The best way to end this chapter is by pointing the reader to the best resources for faith in God. These resources are rich and varied, as has been shown—from the stars of the heavens overhead, visible to the end of creation, and from all that lies within the created world. This universe does have God's unmistakable, infinite fingerprints upon it.

While the heavens declare God's glory, we must still turn to the Lord Jesus Christ to solve our problem of sin and human brokenness. And that's exactly what we find in Jesus's death on the cross:

forgiveness. In his rising from the dead, we find God's vindication of his Son's saving work. The Father's final word of approval of all that Jesus said and did comes from his rising triumphantly from the dead and overcoming this world's "wages of sin" (Romans 6:25), our own eternal death. The Bible teaches that we are invited into fellowship with the risen Jesus, who by grace will transfer his new life to us. In other words, this victory in Jesus is ours to claim.

In closing this chapter, I challenge you to turn to the rich resources for faith found in the Bible. Why not read the Gospel of Luke and experiment with God on your own as you read the history of Jesus, asking Jesus who he is and what his coming can mean to you?

I suggest you start here because many seekers for religious truth find in Jesus Christ a revelation of a Power greater than themselves which sets aside the multitudinous other insights and ideas that we discover within our universe. Explore the religious questions for yourself in the Bible. I wish you well.

There remains a most important question yet to be answered, one that comes first in importance but last in our discovery of the living God. Let us dare to ask God: is there eternal life following our life and death in this world?

CHAPTER 8
The Bottom Line: Is There Eternal Life?

W
e have come a long way from our experience of God found in nature. We have looked at the Bible and different scenes in history, seeing God act in time and space. We now pass to another scene that involves our personal destiny.

This time you are taken to the Hall of the Presidents at Disney World in Florida. Here, you find a brief story of the political history of the United States. Our speaker is an animated model of Abraham Lincoln, who addresses the audience in a speech following the bloodbath of the American Civil War of over a hundred years ago. Reflecting on the significance of human life, especially when facing death, President Lincoln observes, "Man was not made for a day. No, man was made for immortality!"

Surely this is the bottom line of all the questions we can ask of God. People inevitably ask whether there is a life beyond death; it is the one question that matters more than anything else in terms of one's personal destiny.

Dr. Billy Graham, early in his career, had a personal visit with the former Chancellor of West Germany, Conrad Adenhauer. As soon as Dr. Graham entered the room, Adenhauer turned to him and asked him earnestly:"Young man, do you believe in the resurrection of Jesus Christ?'

"I most certainly do," he replied.

"So do I. If Jesus Christ is not risen from the dead, there is not one glimmer of hope for the human race. When I leave office, I'm going to spend the rest of my life studying and writing about the resurrection of Jesus Christ. It's the most important event in human history," Chancellor Adenauer said to Billy Graham.[82]

This is the quintessential question that people with terminal illnesses ask of their ministers, especially if they haven't worked through their religious beliefs before their illness. "What lies ahead? Is there really a God great enough who will grant me personal survival? Is there eternal life, and what will it be like?"

And certainly, at the time of dying, people want to receive the gift of eternal life. This question could be the most important one that we can ask. It is not just an afterthought tacked on at the end of a discussion of religion, for our beliefs about immortality color all of the rest of life and determine what we live for and what we value most.

We see this especially in people who have had near-death experiences, who sometimes report having seen scenes of heaven or even of hell. These experiences can be so vivid and compelling that they change the entire course of their lives.

At this point, we are operating under the belief that the God who created this world also entered it in the form of Jesus Christ. Any question of eternal life must go back to this God as he has disclosed himself to us in Jesus Christ as reported in the Bible. So what does a Christian minister tell dying patients about the possibility of eternal life after death?

Essentially, he tells them that people live two lives. There is the life made up of the senses—touch, taste, sight, hearing, and speech—which is measured in days and years and consists of this passing show of earthly life. But there is another life which overlaps with this earthly life, a life that for believers goes beyond death into a new, deeper, and broader realm of life in the kingdom of heaven.

The minister often tells the dying patient that to die is like getting up from the sickbed and walking through the doorway into a new realm of experience and life in the next room. It is to leave sickness and weakness behind and to pass beyond even death itself into the unseen kingdom of the reign of God.

In this regard, the minister is very much like a train conductor. The minister prepares the dying patient for departure on the train to a distant station. They are given hope, courage, and comfort for their time of departure. Often, they need help to cope with anger at having to leave their loved ones or their present stage of life, or with fear of losing control at the hour of leaving. And there is also the grief of the survivors, who continue on their journey and who may feel helpless to assist their loved ones when they need it most, upset at having to give them up to death—that final debarkation to another place that seems to put a painful distance between the living and the dead.

A BODY WITHOUT BREATH

The concept of the soul or personal identity leaving the body at the point of death is a very ancient belief. It is not only traced back to Socrates of Greek antiquity, but also to communities of *homo sapiens* as far back as we have artifacts of burial.

Beliefs in an afterlife are also very old, for some of the ancient Jewish writers of the Old Testament also affirmed the personal survival of death in which the dead go to be with God in heaven.

What the ancient Hebrews of the Old Testament observed when someone died was that *something* left the body. And that something was, noticeably, breath. In the biblical story, this makes sense: what leaves the body is the divine gift of breath given in the creation of a man that made him a living being in the first place, as recorded in the opening chapters of Genesis. The Jewish authors called the breath the "spirit" of the person. The Hebrew word is the same for both *breath* and *spirit: ruach*. And this breath or spirit was a sign of life within; at death, the person's spirit had departed for another place. Often, writers in the Old Testament thought of the dead person's spirit as going into a shadowy resting place for the dead called *Sheol*.

Although they are few, there are also explicit references in the Old Testament to a heavenly existence *with* God after death. We find one in Psalm 49:13–15 (NIV):

This is the fate of those who trust in themselves . . .

Like sheep they are destined for the grave,

And death will feed on them.

The upright will rule over them in the morning;

their forms will decay in the grave,

Far from their princely mansions.

But God will redeem my life from the grave;

He will surely take me to himself.

Another reference to eternal life with God is found in Isaiah 26:19 (NIV):

But your dead will live;

Their bodies will rise.

You who dwell in the dust,

Wake up and shout for joy.

Your dew is like the dew of the morning;

The earth will give birth to her dead.

Throughout the Old Testament, writers added stone by stone to the temple of belief in eternal life with God. As early as in the first book of the Bible, Enoch, who "walked with God," was taken up into heaven because "God took him away" (Genesis 5:24, NIV). Elijah later was assumed into heaven in the same way (2 Kings 2:11).

Or consider many of the psalms of King David and other psalmists. David speaks in Psalm 16:9–11 of his heart being glad and his tongue rejoicing "because God will not abandon me to the grave, nor will God let your Holy One see decay" (NIV). As David said in the 23rd Psalm, "Surely goodness and mercy shall follow me all the days of my life: and I will dwell in the house of the Lord for ever" (KJV). David was longing in his heart for life with God, which endures all adversity, even death itself, and where David would forever dwell in God's eternity in the house of the worship of God.

The Old Testament authors usually put just one small stone in place in the edifice of the belief in eternal life. Yet, they began a process of building which the Master Craftsman, the Lord Jesus Christ, finished when talking with the Sadducees about the resurrection. The Sadducees (who did not believe in a coming resurrection or afterlife) tried to trick Jesus when they asked him whose husband a woman would have in heaven when she had been married to seven men on earth. Jesus said to them:

> Is not this the reason you are wrong, that you know neither the scriptures nor the power of God? . . . Have you not read in the book of Moses . . . I am the God of Abraham, the God of Isaac and the God of Jacob? He is God not of the dead, but of the living; you are quite wrong. (Mark 12:18, 24, 26–27)

When Jesus said that God was the God of the living and not of the dead, he was only expressing the finishing cornerstone to the concept of an afterlife which is seen under construction in many places of the Old Testament.

Thus far, I have described the Hebrew idea of the breath or spirit of a person leaving the body at the time of death, which is what we observe whenever a person passes away. This concept could be considered the "immortality of the soul."

But doesn't the Bible talk about the "resurrection of the body"? At least, that is what is affirmed in documents like the Apostles' Creed: "I believe in the resurrection of the body and the life everlasting." What happens to the body after someone has died?

What the ancient Hebrews observed is the same as what we observe in the funeral home today—an empty body whose soul has left. We are left with only a decaying shell which will return to ashes and dust in the ground. The life has left, and so the survivors decently bury the remains, treating it with dignity because it represents many memories and feelings.

However, the Bible teaches more than the eternal life of the soul: it also teaches that there will be a restoration of the body that is buried. Thus, the belief in the immortality of the soul *alone* is not a totally Christian idea, for biblical "eternal life" includes also the restoration of the body.

How do we bring these concepts together? The traditional Christian understanding is this: at the time of death, the soul first leaves the body into a kind of disembodied existence. The standard of faith for many Reformed churches around the world, The Westminster Confession, expresses it in these words:

> The bodies of men after death return to dust, and see corruption; but their souls . . . having an immortal substance, immediately return to God who gave them. The souls of the righteous, being then made perfect in holiness are received into the highest heavens, where they behold the face of God in light and glory, waiting for the full redemption of their bodies.[83]

But that last phrase is important: the body will *also* be restored. The time when the body is restored and united in a new way with its soul, for Christians, will occur when at the end of time the Lord Jesus Christ returns to this earth from heaven, coming in glory and power for the judgment of the living and the dead for eternity in heaven or in hell. The consummation of all God's plans for the human race will take place at the time of this final judgment. The Westminster Confession further explains:

> At the last day, such as are found alive shall not die, but be changed: and all the dead shall be raised up with the self-same bodies, and none other, although with different qualities, which shall be united again to their souls for ever.[84]

Thus there will be two stages to eternal life. The first stage is the release of the soul to dwell in the light of God at the point of physical death. The second is the restoration of the body at the end of time, when, as the Bible teaches, the Lord Jesus Christ will return. Jesus said to the thief on the cross at the time of his crucifixion, "Today you will be with me in Paradise." And Paul also taught that to be "away from the body" (to die) is to be "at home with the Lord" (2 Corinthians 5:8). This indicates a disembodied state at this present time, but also a future state of existence when the Bible says believers will have resurrected bodies like that of the Lord Jesus Christ.

THE BODILY APPEARANCE

This may sound like wishful thinking. Isn't it arguments like this that have given philosophers and theologians a bad reputation with the public? Someone once said that a philosopher is a dim-sighted person searching in a dark room for a black cat that isn't there. And a theologian is one who cries out that he's found it!

But there is a rational background for these hopes: the historical resurrection of Jesus. Christians base their great hope in eternal life upon the historical fact that the first disciples personally witnessed the resurrection—the bodily resurrection—of Jesus of Nazareth from the dead. Jesus reveals both the Creator Father and the Creator's plans for resurrection.

The Apostles' Creed says, "He suffered under Pontius Pilate, was crucified, dead, and buried." Christ really *did* die. That crushing day was a sledgehammer blow for the disciples—a sudden, bitter, almost absurd twist of events, totally undeserved, when Jesus was led by the authorities to the Place of the Skull to be nailed to a cross.

Most of us are never fully prepared for a loved one's death. And although Jesus warned his disciples of his coming death, it probably took place too fast for them to fully grasp what was happening. They would have been in a state of shock and disbelief: someone who had said days earlier, "If you have seen me, you have seen the Father," had now been executed by the state. They must have

122 | CONFIDENT FAITH

been completely broken by the sudden death of their Master. Their dreams, fueled by Jesus's teachings during the halcyon days of Galilee and his message of the inbreaking of God's mighty kingdom, would have been dashed and spilled upon the ground like his shed blood. It had every appearance of being over! Their insight into the heart of the universe had been negated and flung insolently back into their faces.

These mourners, now facing an empty future, surely thought the pain of that Friday would never end. Saturday came and went, and that throbbing numbness must have overwhelmed their hearts.

At dawn on Sunday, the third day, several women made their way through the streaks of morning light to the garden tomb where they thought the dead body of Jesus lay. The tomb had been sealed with a large stone, and Roman guards had been stationed there.

Maybe it was a perfect Palestinian morning, when the air was cool and the bright sun poured out its healing warmth. The hearts of these women might have been apprehensive and deeply troubled at the prospect of seeing their Master's dead body once more.

They arrived—and here unfolds a scene of uncertainty and surprise. The stone had been rolled away from the grave. The guards had fled away. And the women were told by two glorious messengers (Greek *angeloi*, meaning messengers or angels) that Jesus was not there. He had risen from the dead! They were to tell the others this good news.

The Gospel of John includes a personal story about the meeting of Mary Magdalene with the risen Lord at the garden. Mary approached one whom she thought was the gardener to ask him where he had placed the body of the dead Jesus. She didn't understand that Jesus had risen from death, for all she could see through her tears was an empty grave. Here is the encounter:

"Woman," Jesus said, "why are you crying? Who is it you are looking for?"

"Sir, if you have carried him away, tell me where you have put him, and I will get him."

Jesus said to her, "Mary." She turned toward him and cried out in Aramaic, "Rabboni!" (which means teacher). Jesus said, "Do not hold on to me, for I have not yet returned to the Father. Go instead to my brothers and tell them, 'I am returning to my Father and your Father, to my God and your God.'" (John 20:10–17, NIV)

The world will never hear any better news than this, given on that first Easter morning! And what better place is there for hearing good news than at a graveside? That gospel, good news, rings throughout the entire world's deep silence: "He is risen!" Jesus, coming from the inner life of God, assumed our humanity and reached as low as we will ever go, to death itself, and has been raised victorious with a new and glorified human body!

This is Christianity at the center. Here we meet the total victory God invites his world to enter. This witnessed appearance of the risen Jesus forms the launching pad for belief in eternal life and our hopes for all creation, which has been subject to decay and death but which now has the promise of restoration and renewal at the end of the age. The Bible rings out in peals of bells to a world dying for the lack of such a positive faith:

Death has been swallowed up in victory. O death where is your victory? O death where is your sting? (1 Corinthians 15:54–55, NIV)

But let us notice that Jesus possessed at his resurrection a special body. It is what the Gospels describe as both a *risen* and a *glorified* human body.

According to the gospel accounts, Jesus possessed a real body in much the same sense as he had before his death. The nail wounds in his hands and the spear wound in his side could actually be touched by the hand of the doubting Thomas. Jesus ate fish and bread at the lakeside with his disciples when he appeared while they were fishing.

But it was also a glorified body. He could do extraordinary things, such as appear before his disciples in the upper room despite the door being shut and bolted from the inside before he appeared. And on the Emmaus Road, he suddenly left the two traveling companions with whom he had journeyed that day after breaking bread with them over dinner and opening their eyes to the fact that he was the risen Lord indeed.

Jesus possessed the same crucified body laid in the tomb; but he had new qualities as well, belonging to his glorified and risen body. And when he departed from his followers forty days later, he added the properties of possessing an ascended body when he *ascended* to heaven.

CLUES FROM WISHFUL THINKING

We can discover a truth from the forcefulness of wishful thinking: when people are confronted with their own mortality, they often find that they cannot face it at all without denial of one sort or another. But what some may consider as only wishful thinking can truly help us cope with the most painful realities of life. We must remember that even our cherished wishes and dreams can tell us something about the nature of reality.

One of North America's most colorful and controversial rabbis, Abraham Feinberg, resigned his pulpit in a prestigious synagogue in New York in 1930 with a nationally debated sermon, a line of which follows:

Organized religion, like the tomb of Tutankhamen, is full of material splendor, but dead —a deserted lighthouse; the tides of human energy beat on other shores.[85]

Feinberg, all his life, was a crusader for unpopular causes. He railed against wars, nuclear power, racism, sexism, ageism, and poverty, although he later served in pulpits across Canada and the United States, including an official position in a Methodist church in San Francisco!

In his eighty-seventh year in 1985, battling cancer of the liver, Feinberg was finally able to accept his mortality. He reflected long and hard on his faith in an omnipotent God while balancing that belief with the existence of evil and his personal fate of a "lingering illness, decay and final extinction," as he described it.

During his ordeal, he sat in his living room reflecting deeply on his need for a solution to his personal crisis. Unable to read books, he considered one solution after another which could give him confidence. His outlook was bleak. Rabbi Feinberg spoke of this searching:

> I'm a rabbi—why couldn't I find solace in the tenets of religion? I touched immortality. I forced myself to be-lieve in immortality. I have a right to do that because we do not know.[86]

Ignorance itself became, for him, a cornerstone of his faith. "Why then complain?" Feinberg concluded. "Only because I want intensely, madly, to live—it's that simple."[87]

Why would God give us such a powerful desire without satisfy-ing that desire? Would he give us the desire for food, for air, for rest, for life itself, without giving us the thing which we crave to satisfy it? Wishful thinking can never bring to us what we seek in itself, but surely it can tell us something significant about the greatest realities in life!

The world's great longing for eternal life is answered in time and space at the garden tomb by the bodily resurrection of Jesus Christ from the dead. Christian faith in eternal life is not just a craving for something we do not know about, whether it is there or not. It is founded upon an event which many witnesses have testi-fied to. And that event is based more broadly upon what the Old Testament authors affirmed as our entrance into unending love and worship of God.

Wishes and dreams tell us significant truths about our inner lives and the way we deal with the outer real world. Our deepest yearn-ings for life, abundant and eternal life, surely are also signposts for the presence of the eternal God and God's destiny for his creation.

All the debate and thoughts about eternal life for the Christian come from Christ's resurrection from the dead, God's seal upon the testament he has given to us in other ways.

THE RESURRECTED GROUP OF DISCIPLES

Besides the gospel accounts themselves, what other evidence do we have for the resurrection? To answer that, we must return to the grieving, shattered disciples—who only days later made a complete turnaround. What other reasonable explanation do we have for the lifting of the intense grief that Jesus's followers experienced within days and weeks after his crucifixion?

The Jesus movement would have effectively been crushed by their Master's sudden death. There were only a few dozen of his closest followers left after that terrible Friday, although there were probably many sympathizers all across Judea, hidden because of fear and disillusionment.

Yet this handful of mourners emerged from hiding within weeks—even before the most intense pain of grief would have taken effect, if indeed he were still dead—to proclaim Jesus as the promised Messiah who had risen from the dead! Not only that, but they appear in the Acts of the Apostles, which chronicles their missions, as a confident and powerful group of men and women who went out all across the then-known world "to turn the world upside down" (Acts 17:6) in the name of their risen Lord Jesus Christ.

These first Christians not only gambled their reputations on this belief, but their very lives. They threw away former successes and positions in society for the sake of knowing Jesus Christ, and they chanced martyrdom as persecution against them heated up. Paul makes this very clear to the Christians living at Philippi:

> But whatever things were gain to me, those things
> I have counted as loss for the sake of Christ. More than
> that, I count all things to be loss in view of the surpassing
> value of knowing Christ Jesus my Lord, for whom I have
> suffered the loss of all things, and count them but rubbish
> so that I may gain Christ. (Philippians 3:7–8, NASB)

The only reasonable explanation to account for how and why this disbanded and disheartened group of disciples were rekindled into a passionate, flaming fellowship is to accept their leader's resurrection. Even authors critical of belief in Christ's resurrection, such as Jewish scholar H.J. Schonfield in his book, *The Passover Plot*,[88] account for the disciples' renewed mission in Jesus's name as coming from nothing less than the reappearance of Jesus to his disciples— although Schonfield tries to argue that this was because Jesus had never died in the first place.

The apostle Paul claimed that Jesus's resurrection had worldwide implications for the destiny of all men, women, and children. Jesus was "the firstfruits of those who have fallen asleep" (1 Corinthians 15:20, ESV) and the hope for all who die. Eternal life will be modeled after what we've already seen in Jesus. We have in this original encounter with the risen Jesus something tangible, a key for unlocking the door of the secrets of the kingdom of heaven. What, then, will heaven be like? What lies on that other shore?

WHAT IS HEAVEN LIKE?

What will heaven be like? This is a reasonable question if the central miracle in the Christian religion, that of Christ's resurrection, really took place. But the answer does not involve knowing our personal door number and specific room in our Father's mansion that Jesus talks about in John 14:2–3:

> In my Father's house there are many dwelling places. If it were not so, would I have told you that I go to prepare a place for you? And if I go and prepare a place for you, I will come again and will take you to myself, so that where I am, there you may be also.

The document entitled *Living Faith*, a subordinate standard of faith for The Presbyterian Church in Canada, summarizes the references to heaven in Scripture:

Life in the age to come is pictured in the Bible in different ways:
The father's house,
A new heaven and earth,
A marriage feast,
An unending day,
And especially, as the fullness
Of the kingdom of God.[89]

Each of these illustrations is a different portrait of the heavenly habitation. Or consider the picture we find of heaven in the twenty-first chapter of the last book of the Bible, Revelation. This portrait has been the basis of jokes which arise when someone supposedly has died and has gone to meet St. Peter at the Pearly Gates. As corny as it sounds, this imagery really does have its source in the Bible. According to the book of Revelation, the heavenly city, the New Jerusalem, shall continue forever. It is a dwelling of vast riches, with streets paved with gold, gates of pearls, and every kind of precious stone in its building. There will be nothing lacking in the heavenly kingdom, for there are riches that surpass understanding.

Jesus often spoke about the riches of God's kingdom. At one point Jesus was confronted by a religious, but wealthy, young ruler who asked how to inherit eternal life. Jesus discussed keeping all of God's law, and then he gave the young man this challenge: "Sell everything you have and give to the poor, and you will have treasures in heaven. Then come, follow me." We learn that the young man went away sorrowful because "he was very rich" (Luke 18:22, NIV).

That rich young ruler could very well be a citizen of our own time in the Western world, because he gave up hope in the unending riches of heaven for the sake of his temporal wealth on this decaying earth.

Heaven offers a place of unspeakable joy and spiritual riches beyond our ability to adequately comprehend. As Paul wrote:

What no eye has seen, no ear has heard, no mind has conceived what God has prepared for those who love him. (1 Corinthians 2:9, NIV)

The most glorious reality of heaven comes from its reality as a place of uniting, or reuniting. Entering heaven is an entering into the courts of the living God with unending joy, praise, and fellowship with the Father, Son, and Holy Spirit, and with the unnumbered multitude of others there, fellow citizens in God's kingdom from all times and places. Heaven doesn't just offer a meeting place of the individual believer with God, but much more broadly, the dwelling place of the heavenly host—saints and martyrs and the whole household of the family of God of every age. There, the entire family of God will worship and fellowship in the light of the Triune God that will never set.

Once in a while, we seem to gain a glimpse of what heaven will be like—from a passage of Scripture, a quiet moment with a loved one, or an inspiring and uplifting moment of worship in church. For me, there occurred a special occasion like this at St. John's Convalescent Convent in Toronto one Christmas Eve while at the Midnight Mass. I had been invited by a friend to go before I became an ordained minister. During the time of intercessory prayer offered by each of the nuns, I felt that heaven must be much like this. The candles were softly flickering and silently protesting the dark and cold of the outside winter's night. Incense floated through the chapel. Each of the nuns rose to her feet separately and said prayers for this person or that cause. They prayed for people who might never know they were being lifted up that night to the throne of God for his blessing.

There was a great sense of that "peace of God, which surpasses all understanding" (Philippians 4:7) in the room. And I thought heaven must be something like this: everyone forgetting their sorrow, pain, and selfishness, lost in worship of God and praying for the welfare of others. Here was that wonderful gift of peace, that biblical shalom, which binds human to human and humans to God!

But this is only one portrait of heaven. Each person should have a portrait of his or her own hanging somewhere in the gallery of life's experiences.

But here we come up against limitations. God doesn't let us gaze into heaven for very long. For example, as soon as the Lord Jesus had ascended to heaven, the apostles were asked by two angels, "Men of Galilee, why do you stand here looking up toward Heaven?"(Acts 1:11). They were to stop looking up and contemplating heaven and return to Jerusalem to carry out the work of their mission. Their ancient world was longing and waiting to know all about the confident faith the apostles had discovered in the life, death, and resurrection of Jesus Christ!

Sometimes an artist's painting or even a comic in a weekend newspaper can capture something of a significant religious truth. This cartoon by Bil Keane struck me as illustrating from a child's perspective something of the household of the faith.[90]

Although our images are always inadequate to fully portray reality, they can still be helpful and uplifting.

LIFE IN THE FOURTH DIMENSION

The problem with gaining detailed knowledge of heaven is that we are talking about a different dimension of existence than the three dimensions we normally see. We measure and know everything in our world according to length, breadth, and depth. We cannot adequately imagine the fourth dimension of the Holy Spirit and the place of God's heaven, just as it would be difficult for a person having information in only two dimensions to imagine that same thing in three.

Just imagine someone who had never seen a human being, but who saw the handprint of a man on a dusty tabletop. From this solitary handprint in the two dimensions of length and width, could this person ever imagine a real human being in three dimensions of length, width, and depth standing on his feet? It hardly seems possible. So how can we humans ever adequately imagine heaven, which exists in the fourth dimension of the Spirit and the heavenly?

We can't—however, we are given precious glimpses of these mysteries.

There is the story of a wise doctor who visited the chronic care wing of the hospital on Saturdays because that was the only day which his busy schedule allowed. And he would always come in the company of his five-year-old son, who would wait for him in the visitor's lounge on the ground floor.

One patient in the chronic wing had just heard that he was dying and longed for someone to talk to him about whether heaven existed or not, and what it would be like. But no one was available. Finally, he thought, "I'll ask my wise doctor when he comes to visit on Saturday."

As was his custom, the doctor came to visit the next Saturday and left his son downstairs. When he entered the room, the dying man said to him, "Doctor, I want to know if there is a heaven and what it will be like. I have no one to ask and wondered if you could tell me something about this?"

The doctor hesitated a few moments and then said, "I'm not really the one to ask. I know so little."

"Then please tell me what you do know, Doctor," the patient earnestly requested. "I trust your opinion, and I know you can answer my question."

Just then, there was a tiny knocking at the door of the patient's room, and the doctor knew that this day his son had come up the stairs by himself and followed him to this room.

The doctor's eyes brightened as he now tried to answer the man's questions. "That is my son who is knocking on your door. He has never been in this room before and has no idea of anything that is in here. He cannot even imagine what your room is like. But he is not afraid of what is on the other side of the door, because he knows his father who loves him is waiting for him there."

The unique gift of the Christian faith to the world comes from Jesus, who has shown humanity the love of the Father who is on the other side of death. Because of that, we can trust God for whatever in this world of joy or sorrow, life or death, awaits us.

WHERE IS GOD IN THE STORM?

We have presented the case for the First Cause and the Intelligent Designer being visible in Jesus Christ—for seeing God visibly in Jesus's words and miraculous deeds, in the testimony of others to him, and in his death and resurrection. Also, we have looked at the case for eternal life. But there is one other place we must be able to see God if Jesus is Lord: that is, if he is Immanuel, "God with us." That place is in our own storms of life.

On our tours to the Holy Land, we take a boat ride on the Sea of Galilee where Jesus's disciples were fishermen. Out about two miles from shore, we can see in the distance the north shore where Jesus fed the five thousand with two fish and five barley loaves. The church marking that spot, Tabga, is seen off in the distance there.

Out on the lake, we can feel the wind blowing from the southwest across the greatest expanse of the lake, from which the prevailing winds blow. And they remind us of another story. One extremely stormy night, after Jesus had dismissed the crowd of five thousand that had been miraculously fed at Tabga, the disciples tried to cross the lake and got to about this spot where the waves and winds were most severe. These experienced sailors feared that their lives were in extreme peril and that they would not survive the night.

Then, struggling in the boat with all their might, they saw a shadowy figure coming to them on the water in the dim light of morning. "Look!" Peter shouted to the others in the boat. "It's—it's a ghost!" Surely this was an omen of the end of their lives!

But it was Jesus walking to them on the water. Jesus immediately spoke to them and said, "Take heart, it is I; do not be afraid" (Matthew 14:27). Jesus rebuked the tempestuous winds and waves, and calm came over the lake. "And those in the boat worshiped him, saying, 'Truly you are the Son of God'"(Matthew 14:33).

Jesus saved his disciples that day from a terrible storm. And this brings us to the final place where we must look for God. It seems that no one in this world is immune from storms, whether financial hardship, health issues, conflict with loved ones, broken relationships, or injustice. In fact, it is the storms in life that appear to be the greatest obstacle to faith for many atheists and unbelievers. Perhaps menacing storms have been the greatest obstacle for you too.

"How can there be a God if there is such immense suffering in the world?" you question. "If there is a God, he must be a heartless tyrant or a diabolical demon to allow a world of suffering like this!" many say. A theodicy for this—an explanation answering the pain of suffering—is difficult to find and too often unsatisfactory.

I have also faced painful storms that have drained the life and faith out of me. I want to end this book by showing you that in my fiercest storms, God has been visibly and audibly present in Jesus Christ to calm it. I have heard his words in the storm saying to me as he did on the Sea of Galilee that terrible night, "Take heart, it is I; do not be afraid."

I want you to see the living God in suffering as I tell you my story.

PART 3

God in Storms

CHAPTER 9
My Story

It was the lowest point in my whole life. I could hardly sit still in the balcony of the Peoples' Church for the Sunday morning worship service in Toronto. Both my legs were shaking from the side effects of the old-fashioned psychotropic medication my doctor had put me on. But I was able to listen carefully to what was being said.

A woman minister in charge of counseling stood at the platform to lead in the prayers for the congregation. She prefaced her prayers with opening words I will never forget: "We believe in a miracle-answering God who hears and answers prayer!"

That was all I needed to hear in church at that time in my wounded life. I closed my eyes and silently cried out to God with all my heart: "God, I don't know if I ever will get out of this hole that I am in. I don't know if I will ever graduate with my MA, or if I will ever get a job as a minister, or if, dear God, I will ever get married. But please, dear, dear God, help me to get out of this terrible pit that I am in!"

How did I ever fall into such a desperate situation?

After my second year at Edinburgh, I should have spent the summer brushing up on my Latin and Greek and the early church fathers before returning for my third year in the Honors Bachelor of Divinity degree in 1970. But that summer I worked hard making money on construction. I thought I would finish my divinity degree at Knox College, at the University of Toronto, home seminary of my denomination.

My plans took a turn when the principal at Knox, J. Stanley Glen, advised me to complete my degree at New College in Edinburgh. When I arrived back in Scotland, I was almost a month late starting the third honors year. The catching up was enormous work. I remember working in the residence library after the bars got out on Prince's Street below me at 1 a.m. and hearing them singing on their way home. It was even necessary to work through the holidays.

THE MARKS WERE POSTED

It almost all paid off. The marks were posted, and I was hoping to have grades adequate to enter a PhD program at Harvard University in Boston. I scanned the board, and there was my name—but the average was one level short of what I needed. I couldn't believe it as I read and reread the board.

With this posting, something inside me broke. I didn't know what to do. I had worked so hard, putting every single thing I had in me on this one peg, and now the peg had broken!

I went for a walk down High Street from the Mound toward Holyrood Palace, the queen's Scottish residence. And with every step down the hill, my heart sank lower and lower. Even when I got home that summer, I couldn't pull out of my sadness and gloom. Nothing seemed to cheer me up.

I began a master's program in September at Knox College, but what I really needed was a job with other workers, recreation, and pleasurable conversations, not more intense academic work. My concentration was severely diminished by Christmas. And on a forced visit by my residence don to the university health clinic, I was told that I needed to go for treatment at the hospital immediately. I couldn't accept that I needed help, and I quickly walked out of the doctor's office.

Having nowhere to go, I wandered aimlessly on Yonge Street in Toronto until I was stopped by the police. They made some phone calls and found that I needed to be taken to a brand-new psychiatric hospital on the edge of campus, the Clarke Institute. When I realized I was being admitted as a patient, I struggled with all my might to leave that place, ending up being wrestled to the ground by four psych assistants. As I was a strong athlete—a star water polo player for my college—the assistants were greatly challenged to bring me under control! They gave me a massive dose of tranquilizers, and I slept for two days.

The psychiatrist entered my room several days after that and said to me, "Larry, you may not know what has happened to you, but you have had what is called a nervous breakdown. You will get better and probably make a full recovery, but you will have to take medication to help you from now on into the future."

I recovered very quickly and returned to my studies. But I also went off the pills the doctor had prescribed for me.

Four month later, I had an even more serious relapse and voluntarily returned to the Clarke. I suffered now from severe depression, and I underwent four treatments of electroconvulsive therapy (electric shock treatment). It did seem to help.

MASTERING TEN MINUTES, YOU CAN MASTER A RECOVERY

Recovery this time only happened when they put me on a strong regimen of medication, but that also made everything much more difficult. Not knowing how I would ever sit still long enough to go to work in the library to finish my master's degree, I decided I would time myself on my watch. I would try to sit in the library for exactly ten minutes and then immediately go back to the Clarke. The next day I made it twelve, then fifteen, and in several weeks, thirty minutes. Within a year, I could spend two hours or more studying in the library.

Hope can be found for almost any condition, I have found, if a person can master and succeed for ten minutes at a time! The slightest effective exertion, even if lasting only for a few minutes, can lead to a complete recovery when combined with continued effort, encouragement from others, and certainly help from almighty God in answer to prayer. When things seemed almost impossible for me, mastering ten minutes at a time led to a complete recovery in my life! Prayer was key to my recovery as well.

A skeptic might suggest that my answered prayer at Peoples' Church was just a coincidence or a matter of good luck. To that, I say this: if all we knew about God was that he was the First Cause of creation, or even that he is creation's Intelligent Designer, then there might not be any way to know if a recovery like mine was a response of God in answer to prayer.

However, when we put into context all that we know about God's unveiled power to Israel in the Old Testament and the visible coming of the Lord Jesus Christ in the New—whom many people still find today to be the "Great Physician" painted in the Bible—then we can be certain that it is God who is at work.

In this context of knowing God in nature and from the best of our human history, it is clear to me that my heart's deepest longings were answered by God's direct, interactive touch of grace in my wounded life. God has always been interactive with me, guiding and answering prayer.

Someone may ask, "How long do you have to pray for this to work?" The answer comes, how strong do you want to be spiritually and physically? Now, after a lifetime of "praying without ceasing," as the apostle Paul urged believers to do (1 Thessalonians 5:17), I have found God continuously giving strength and blessing, even at the greatest times of crisis, in answer to prayer.

Still to this day, when leading in prayers in church, I often say to people what I heard at the Peoples' Church in 1973: "We believe in a miracle-answering God who hears and answers prayer!" The prayer I said in church that Sunday morning was truly answered by God, though not until almost exactly twenty years later. I encourage people today to be patient with God, for he does hear our prayers and knows the best timing and the best gifts to give in answer to our hearts' desires.

The storm that brought me down and almost destroyed my life in 1971 continued to roar in my life during those early years of recovery. The doctors diagnosed my condition years later as occasional cycles of depression and exultation. (Today, no one would ever suspect any mood disorder in my very stable life!)

It was sometime during those early months of recovery at the Clarke that I went to the Peoples' Church in Toronto and prayed my prayer for recovery. When I got discharged from the Clarke, I worked as a journalist for several years. Then, briefly, I worked as a student chaplain at a Boys Training School, ending up later that year as a supervisor of men at the Salvation Army's Minimum Security Jail at the House of Concord, north of Toronto, in 1976.

In those early years of 1976–1980, the problem was still so intense that I began to despair of life itself. I dwelt on the thought of what a relief it would be to just die and leave this world. But I could never plan anything deliberate because the thought was always in my mind, "What a terrible example that would be for my family to think that I couldn't solve my problems and killed myself! What would they do if they ever faced problems like mine?"

I knew I couldn't continue to dwell on dying. One night at the beginning of winter, I was on my rounds and entered the weight room at the House of Concord. I saw how hard these incarcerated men worked to stay fit and how they were training for the long term.

"That's what I need," I told myself. "God, please help me to not think again about dying for at least two years. If my problem isn't any better after two years, then I don't care what happens to me."

I felt I had made a legitimate deal with God. I put all those thoughts of dying out of my mind, and in fact, I never did know when those two years were up because things continued to get better and better. Every time my problem knocked me down, it was my faithful and loving God who always helped me to get back up on my feet and start over again!

BACK TO THE FUTURE AGAIN

In 1981, I was ordained into the Presbyterian Church in Canada and began serving the two churches of Chalmers and Knox, Jarvis, in the Hamilton Presbytery in southern Ontario. Finally my life was in gear once again.

In 1983, I met Karen Ebert, who would come home to her mother's church across town on weekends and help with our joint young peoples' groups. We fell in love and were married August 11, 1984. Karen advised me that if I had any further plans to do postgraduate studies, I'd better begin immediately before we started a family.

That fall, I started my doctoral work at the University of Toronto's Knox College, a four-year program. In 1989 I published my first book, *The Gamble of Faith*,[91] and graduated with my doctorate, and in 1990, Karen and I had our Confederation Log Home built on the sandy shores of Lake Erie, overlooking Erie, Pennsylvania, across the lake. We have enjoyed a wonderful marriage, and in those first six years, both of us spent a great deal of time every weekday morning studying the Bible and praying together.

There are times in life when a series of interrelated events work so well, so marvelously, that you know these events are directly the work of God in your life. More miraculous times were yet to come.

Our plans and dreams were to start a family right away when we got married, but we had all sorts of problems, and we did everything from surgery to fertility medication and the programs at the clinic in London, Ontario. Nothing was happening for us.

In the summer of 1990, Karen and I were walking down the marina road at my father's summer cottage in Muskoka, talking longingly about our desire to have a family. For many reasons, we felt hopeless, and we were in tears as we talked together. I said to Karen,

"Don't worry, Karen, I can see how God has gifted you in raising children with the way you treat the children of our family and friends. I don't believe God would have given you this gift without giving us children to raise."

We could hardly believe the speed at which God answered our heart's desire that same year! Now we have two grown daughters, Alena and her younger sister Erika, who both love the Lord and are active in the church. We had no doubt at all that this blessing of family came right from our loving God who hears and answers prayer!

Then, in February 2002, I was traveling home from Toronto from Pine Ridge Presbyterian Church where I had served for ten years, as well as traveling as an international evangelist for the last nineteen years. Thoughts were going over and over in my mind about something television personality David Mainse had been saying to me for several years: "Larry, why don't you start a television program on our new station, Crossroads Television System?"

That winter's night on the highway home, I remembered a program that had been hosted by a man named Terry Winters until his untimely death at an early age brought his show to an end. No one had reduplicated the format. Could I do a show like his, with a twenty-minute interview with a Christian leader and a closing seven-minute commentary inviting the viewer to know Jesus Christ presented by our guest? I turned the idea over and over in my mind that night on my way home on the 401 Highway.

The president of CTS, Dick Gray, was very enthusiastic about the idea, and he led me to an excellent producer, Mr. Michael Hanley, a former producer of *100 Huntley Street* and one of Canada's most talented Christian producers! When we raised the entire budget for the first year in advance, my board of directors approved going ahead to air the show.

Our thirty-minute program, *Reachout for Life*, began in September 2003 and is still reaching many hundreds of thousands of viewers. It airs four times a week across all of Canada, seen on affiliate stations in the U.S and internationally, and streamed live, worldwide, on the Internet. It can now also be viewed on the Miracle Channel. Karen and I had founded Reachout Ministries as an international evangelistic ministry in 1992, and all of us see so clearly the strong hand of God working through every detail of the *Reachout for Life* television program.

In just the last few years, God laid his guiding hand upon me again, working out all the details with accuracy and speed as he led Karen, the girls, and me to a new pastoral charge at St. Paul's Presbyterian Church in Burlington, Ontario. We face the challenge of being in a fast-growing region of Burlington North. Again, we see no mistake in God's leading us here—not as chance or good luck, but through the unmistakable hand of a gracious God who delights in leading his people.

With my miraculous recovery from a serious illness, our daughters coming into our family, God's guiding hand taking us to St. Paul's, and seeing many answers to daily prayed-for needs, I know from experience that the words of Jesus are trustworthy and true when he said, "Ask and it will be given you; search and you will find; knock, and the door will be opened for you" (Matthew 7:7).

You can test and prove God's faithfulness for yourself. These words that Jesus spoke are his invitation to you to genuinely experiment and prove him to be true. You can find this God who hears and answers your prayers in Jesus Christ.

A MOMENT THAT CHANGES DESTINY

What a difference a single step can make! Throughout my life, seemingly inauspicious steps, without my awareness of any kind of consequence to come, have proven able to change everything when that one step comes from God and goes in God's direction.

To use a commonly repeated Chinese proverb, a journey of a thousand miles begins with a single step. For me, the single step took every ounce of strength and courage I had, but that first ten minutes in the library radically changed my whole world. It entirely changed my destiny, and the consequences of that are still being worked out in my beloved nation of Canada.

Ten minutes! That's an almost insignificant period of time. Yet it was one solitary footstep in the right direction.

Brief momentary events can change the entire outcome of history. This is seen in the stories of many great leaders. Fyodor Dostoevsky is one example. A brilliant writer, Dostoevsky wrote some of the most profound books on good and evil, and crime and punishment, not only in Russian literature but also on the world stage.

At twenty-five years of age, Dostoevsky captured the hearts of Russia with his famed novel *Poor Folk*. This success led the celebrated young novelist to excessive partying, drinking, and a careless outburst of criticism against the Russian czar. He was arrested and condemned by the court to death by a firing squad. As the blindfold was tightened over his eyes, he heard the guns being cocked, but there came the sounds of running footsteps. The czar had commuted the sentence to ten years of hard labor—but so severe was this last moment's reprieve for Dostoevsky that he suffered an epileptic seizure, the onset of a condition that would last the rest of his life.

While he was making the dreadful journey to Omsk in Siberia, an incredibly small gesture happened on Christmas Eve in 1849 that changed his life forever. It came from the seemingly insignificant arrival of a peasant woman who wanted to share something with Dostoevsky that she cherished. She reached her hand through the fence and handed a tiny book into the shaking hand of the prisoner Dostoevsky when his tormentors' backs were turned. She whispered to him, "Read it carefully at your leisure." Just a brief, momentary hand reaching through a fence! What could possibly help Dostoevsky in this frozen desert of pain—with summer days so unbearably hot and winter nights bitterly frigid, biting into his slender body? That book was only a tiny New Testament of the Bible.

Dostoevsky's daughter Aimee tells in her 1921 biography of her father that this New Testament was Dostoevsky's only solace in prison and his greatest treasure for the rest of his life. Ruth Bell Graham quotes Aimee's words in *Prodigals and Those Who Love Them*:

He studied the precious volume from cover to cover, pondered every word; learned much of it by heart, and never forgot it. All his works were saturated with it, and it is this which gives them their power.[92]

A peasant woman's hand shot through a fence, offering a tiny book in secret. Is that all it took to save a life? Just a moment's gesture—but so immense was that tiny volume that it became the turning point in the career of one of the world's greatest novelists. Like the rising sun melting the arctic winter, Dostoevsky discovered in this little volume a way to endure the bitterness of life's worst in that wretched prison camp in Siberia.

A common peasant.

A hand through the fence.

A tiny book.

A secret moment.

Yet something here was great enough to change Dostoevsky's life and work and the world of literature!

THE CALLING OF AN EVANGELIST

In my own life, another tiny step with huge consequences occurred when my wife Karen and I drove to Columbia, North Carolina, for a Billy Graham Crusade and School of Evangelism in 1987. The night before the school began, we huddled in Brice-Taylor football stadium to attend the crusade meeting. As Canadians, we were expecting the southern U.S. warmth, but we had to pull our jackets close against a chilly spring wind. The music was great, and Dr. Graham had a well-prepared and powerfully delivered sermon. Afterward, we said how good it was to be there that night.

Then, after a day at the school, we had to make observations at the crusade service as part of our homework. However, this night stirred the soul for both Karen and me. As we sat there and watched the playing field below fill with those making commitments, Karen expressed something I too longed for but didn't have the courage to ask. "Larry, we should go forward to rededicate our future work in the ministry to the Lord."

"I would love to, Karen," I quietly replied, "but already everyone has gone forward. Let's do it tomorrow night."

The next night, we were joined by friends from the School of Evangelism and couldn't find an opportunity to go forward. The night after that, Karen and I sat by ourselves close to the field where the platform stood. When Dr. Graham gave the invitation, Karen and I were two of the first to stand in our area and make our way forward.

Karen and I were both counseled by Bible college students. My young counselor said, "You're a what? A minister from Canada?" and a little later, "You're a what? A student studying at the University of Toronto for your doctorate? Tell me," he asked, "why did you come forward?"

"I want to give my life to the Lord Jesus Christ without any conditions for my work and ministry in the days ahead for the rest of my life!" I answered. The young counselor then closed with a strong prayer of dedication to the Lord.

Something unforeseen and unexpected happened when Karen and I returned to our room at the Holiday Inn. That night, Karen was reading on the bed, and I was reading Psalm 37 and praying at the desk. In warm conversation with the Lord, I read Psalm 37:4: "Delight yourself in the Lord, and He will give you the desires of your heart" (NIV). I recalled my heart's desire in Mr. Cooper's Bible study class in high school to someday become an evangelist. In my Canadian Presbyterian denomination, there is no training for this, and that desire had eluded me all along as I had been able to train only for a career as a minister, a chaplain, or a professor in seminary.

That night, God had looked upon my steps to go forward. God knew that he now had my ears open. "Larry," God's silent conversation spoke in my heart, "you have always desired in your heart to serve me as an evangelist. Now that you have responded and have given me your life, I want you to serve me now as an evangelist and call many other people to commit their lives to me as you did tonight!"

I would never have had open ears to hear this call from God unless I had taken those few small steps down the stadium ramp to open my life to God's leading! I knew this was from God. Again, something brief and momentary was happening, much like ten minutes in the library, that was changing the direction of my entire life. Now God had placed an irrevocable call upon my life, not just as a pastor, but also as an evangelist.

Karen and I were changed servants of God when we got back to Chalmers and Knox, Jarvis, in the spring of 1987—but we weren't ready to launch out into the deep waters of evangelism yet. By 1990, we had our family well started with our daughters Alena and Erika, and we had our "retirement" Confederation Log Home on the shores of Lake Erie, but we didn't resign and start service in Reachout Ministries as evangelists until November 1, 1992.

On that first day of November as we took our first step into a new calling, all our money was spent, and I had no bookings for speaking, but I could do a little high school supply teaching. Karen and I had saved about one thousand dollars to spend on advertising our new evangelistic ministry. Now there came a great problem: we felt we needed to help with a different cause.

David Mainse, founder and host of Canada's longest running and most widely viewed Christian television show, *100 Huntley Street*, was in desperate financial condition because of a tragic recession during Spain's World Fair that had lost his ministry tens of millions of dollars. We were faithful viewers of his program and saw how little good it would do for our ministry to use that one thousand dollars and how much more it would bless *100 Huntley Street* in their great work for the Lord.

I walked into David's Mainse's office at the Crossroads center and handed David the check for the full amount. David was surprised and asked me to come back the next morning to give the gift on the air. I did and made an impassioned plea to the television audience: "This check comes from a very dear cause we have been saving for, but *100 Huntley Street* is more important. I appeal to all of you watching today, if you have been saving money for a new TV, or a special dream vacation, or a new appliance, now is the time to help David. Please, just like Karen and I did, send your largest and most sacrificial check to David today!"

I don't know how much it helped, but *100 Huntley Street* over the next few years did survive that financial storm and is stronger today than ever! I had no expectations from this gift other than helping Canada's most significant ministry at a difficult time. This small step could bode no benefit for us as far as we could see.

The next year, Karen and I went to Louisville, Kentucky, for the North American Conference of Itinerant Evangelists. I had the honor to meet and get to know Canada's best-known evangelist, Dr. John Wesley White, who asked us several times how he could help us as a young evangelistic ministry.

The following year, I had no idea at the time about the chemistry going on between these two great national leaders. David Mainse and John Wesley White were scheduling six evangelistic crusades with world evangelists, every other month for one week each, on the live television program *100 Huntley Street*. John recommended my name, and David immediately responded with enthusiasm.

My turn was the last among many leading world evangelists in a series that ran over Remembrance Day in 1994. The challenge for me was not in making a twenty-eight-minute sermon long enough for live television but in making it no shorter than exactly twenty-eight minutes!

David Mainse as host, the music, the studio audience, and all those making decisions for Christ still remain in my memory as one of the highlights of my life. In fact, it confirmed God's calling upon my life as an evangelist, because when I saw the number of those calling in on the phone lines for all six evangelists, I learned that my week of ministry had the second largest number of those calling in decisions for Christ during the telecast, actually tying in second place with the legendary Rex Humbard.

Birth of a Ministry

God's domino effect in my life was now in full process. A step forward in a stadium led to a call from God to become an evangelist. Then a single check to one man and an introduction to another provided the divine chemistry for a week of evangelistic ministry on live national television on the Global Network.

God now had positioned me where he wanted me to be, and he was about to turn my blessings into much greater fruitfulness. David Mainse had several times urged me to start a television ministry on the CTS network, as I have already shared. The call to be an evangelist in North Carolina and the successful week of television ministry on *100 Huntley Street* came together in 2003 as God led me to become an evangelist and television host of my international interview program, *Reachout for Life*.

God keeps doing great things in both Canada and the United States, where we see Christian leaders emerging in all areas of life[93] (some of whom have been interviewed on our television program in Canada). These Christian leaders all testify to the undeniable evidence for God that they have found in a personal relationship with Jesus Christ. God offers this same relationship to you as well—it is God's free gift, if you are willing.

The hardest part for me was giving to the Lord that first ten minutes in the library and then taking three or four additional steps on a longer journey that offers yet even greater possibilities! If *you* are willing, *God is always willing* to help you take that all-important first step toward him and then toward your goals.

Zacchaeus Climbs Up a Tree

The Bible shows us in many places the tremendous significance of a single step taken toward God. One of my favorite encounters in the Bible, in Luke 19:1–10, tells of the steps that a tax collector by the name of Zacchaeus took in climbing a tree to see Jesus pass by. An ancient sycamore tree, possibly the very one Zacchaeus climbed, still stands in modern-day Jericho. As Luke tells the story, Jesus and a large entourage were passing by on their way to Jerusalem for the high feast of the Passover. Zacchaeus, who was very rich—probably from dishonest tax revenue charged to the people of his city—nevertheless wanted to see this Jesus. Being short in stature, he had to take a few steps up the sycamore tree beside the main road going through Jericho.

A minister friend of mine with whom I have worked, the Reverend Samir Aboukeer, loves to point out that no one wanting to find and meet Jesus will ever be disappointed. Jesus saw Zacchaeus in the tree and called for him to come down. Jesus invited himself and his twelve disciples to Zacchaeus's home for the day. Over the meal, Zacchaeus discovered for himself what many in Judea had also found in Jesus. The presence of God entered into Zacchaeus's home, and in response, Zacchaeus vowed to give away half his fortune and repay any wrongs he had done. Jesus assured this tax collector, who had been expelled from the synagogue, that he too was a true Israelite and that today salvation had come into his home!

That change all began for Zacchaeus when he took a few steps up a climbable sycamore tree. Ten minutes in the library devoted to the Lord, or a few steps toward God, not only can change lives, it can change history.

If you are willing to take those steps forward in the right direction, that is, toward the Lord Jesus Christ, you will find a new life that will impact your family, your career, and even your nation. You can always find a confident faith in God by going to the Jesus Christ. Creation and design are great prompters for faith, but ultimately Jesus is all you will ever need to know to find the living God and the true life he alone can give! God blesses everyone who will give him ten good minutes and a few faithful steps!

WHERE JESUS IS MOST REAL

The last chapter ended with a storm on the Sea of Galilee. Just as the disciples were rescued from imminent peril on the furious lake that early morning, it is my testimony that God is willing and able to rescue you in your storms too! God can indeed be seen in nature, and most clearly, God can be seen in the entire Bible, especially in the life, death, and resurrection of the Lord Jesus Christ. Can God also be seen in human suffering? I add my personal witness to that of the disciples on the lake, with a confident faith testifying yes, to you and to the Lord!

But there is one last thing. If you are seeking after God, you may wonder where you can best find him in Jesus Christ. Is it necessary for you to go to the Holy Land, where Jesus lived, died, and was raised again, or to some great center of Christian pilgrimage?

This is not at all true in my experience. I feel the closest to the Lord beside my bed when I pour out my heart's desires to him—or when I pray without ceasing as I drive my car down the road—or anywhere when I turn and call out to him. The reason Jesus is so close *right here at home* is because Jesus is not a dead religious leader buried in some holy place in Israel or present only in religious centers or church buildings. He rose from the dead. So Jesus is most present and most real wherever people are willing to call upon his name! And people do want this kind of faith: I have found over and over again in all my international ministry that the world truly wants to believe.

In finishing this book, you may now feel that you have learned something personal about how the author has found a confident faith in God. More importantly, you may have found yourself coming to believe in *God*, and in the words he has spoken in the Bible. You may be forming a faith, a personal relationship with God. Now it is up to you to explore this relationship, especially by returning to God's further conversation with you in the Bible.

I would love to help you know God more personally by leading you in a prayer that Jesus said the heavenly Father is always willing to hear: "God, be merciful to me a sinner" (Luke 18:13–14). May I add a few more words to this prayer?

"O Lord, I see your fingerprints everywhere in my world, especially in the Bible. I know how far I have fallen from your example, Lord Jesus. Forgive me and give me your gift of love, forgiveness, and eternal life, and the abundant life you want me to have. Help me to go with you now through whatever storms I face and find your strength for this journey. Thank you, Lord. In Jesus's name I pray, amen."

I am sure that God has heard your prayer. Keep looking to the Lord Jesus Christ.

> "For now we see in a mirror dimly, but then we
> will see face to face."
> —The Apostle Paul (1 Corinthians 13:12)

Endnotes

1. Broadcast on *The View*, an ABC television network production, circa 2008.

2. Søren Kierkegaard, *Philosophical Fragments* (Princeton, NJ: Princeton University Press, 1969), 53.

3. John Allen Paulos, *Irreligion: A Mathematician Explains Why the Arguments for God Just Don't Add Up* (New York: Hill and Wang, 2008).

4. Timothy Avery, "One in four don't believe in God, poll finds," *The Toronto Star* (Toronto: Canadian Press) Harris-Decema survey, May 31, 2008, Religion Page.

5. Thomas F. Torrance, *Theological Science* (London: Oxford University Press, 1969).

6. This can be seen in dominant theological works such as Paul Tillich's three-volume *Systematic Theology* and other seminal works like John Baillie's *Our Knowledge of God*.

7. Prof. E.L. Mascall has a number of scholarly works with popular appeal, such as *Existence and Analogy*. Also see Canadian theologian/philosopher Etienne Gilson, who has produced quality publications such as *Being and Some Philosophers*.

8. Northrup Frye, speaking at Victoria University, University of Toronto, c. May 1968.

9. Prof. E.L. Mascall, *He Who Is* (London: Darton, Longman & Todd, 1966), 45. Eric Mascall summarizes the Second Way of Thomas Aquinas:

    "The notion of efficient causality is inevitable as soon as we inquire not merely *how* things happen, but *why*. Events are caused by other events, things have effects upon one another. And the Second Way proceeds by two steps which are closely similar to those in the First. It begins from the assertion that in the world there is an order of efficient causality, an interrelation, sometimes simple, sometimes very complex, of causes and effects. And it then argues that we cannot proceed to infinity in the sequence of efficient causes; there must be a First Cause, which is itself uncaused but is, directly or indirectly, the cause of everything except itself. And to this, concludes St. Thomas, 'everyone gives the name of God.'"

10. St. Thomas's first "proof" for God's existence, his First Way, was from motion, which means not only change of position in space but any kind of change. Everything that moves is put in motion by something else. This series of things in motion is finite, because everything we observe is itself finite and hence the series of things in motion, too, has a prime mover that starts the series which itself must be the cause of its own motion, or can be said to be the unmoved First Mover. Aquinas concludes this is what we mean by God.

    The Second Way for St. Thomas was that of efficient causality. This argument looks at the universe of finite causes and effects going back to God who is the First Cause starting everything.

    The Third Way in Aquinas, the cosmological argument, starts from consideration of the universe in which we all live. This third way is very similar to the first two ways. It argues that in the generation and decay of the physical universe there are a series of unnecessary things that exist since they are transient in life and disappear without any necessity to exist. Now everything cannot be said to be unnecessary like this, because something must necessarily exist or there would be no unnecessary existing things today. If this necessary Being was caused by something else, there would be an eternal series of things, which is impossible. The only thing that necessarily exists is what we mean by God.

The Fourth Way for St. Thomas is the argument from the degrees of being, which is only briefly mentioned in *Summa Contra Gentiles*.

The Fifth Way is that of design. We will give a quite different example of this argument in the next chapter on God's intelligent design in nature, but in Aquinas, what is stressed in the fifth argument is not the First Cause of creation but the Final Cause or design toward which creation is moving. Thus it is called the *teleological argument* (design toward an end).

11. See John Hick, *Philosophy of Religion* (Upper Saddle River, NJ: Prentice Hall, 1964), 20 ff.

12. Henry D. Aiken, *The Age of Ideology* (New York: Mentor, 1956), 36 ff.

13. For a very brief overview of the facts, see http://www.harvard-house.com/universe_to_end.htm.

14. John Allen Paulos, *Irreligion: A Mathematician Explains Why the Arguments for God Just Don't Add Up* (New York: Hill and Wang, 2008), 34 ff.

15. Ibid., 47.

16. Robert Fulford, "From a brilliant mind a silly book," *The National Post*, December 16, 2006, op. ed. page.

17. Alister McGrath, *The Twilight of Atheism* (New York: Doubleday, 2004), 98.

18. T.F. Torrance, *Theology in Reconstruction* (Grand Rapids, MI: William B. Eerdmans, 1965), 109–116.

19. Richard Dawkins, *The God Delusion* (New York: Houghton Mifflin, 2006), 77.

20. Karl Barth, *Church Dogmatics*, Vol. 1 (Edinburgh: T. & T. Clark, 1963), 540.

21. Antony Flew said he had to "follow the evidence of intelligent design" to a Creator God in an interview with Dr. Gary Habermas in the Winter 2004 *Philosophia Christi*. Flew explains his change of belief in *There Is a God: How the World's Most Notorious Atheist Changed His Mind*, coauthored with Roy Abraham Varghese (New York: HarperOne, 2008).

22. Francis Collins in Claudia Wallis, "The Evolution Wars," *TIME*, August 15, 2005, 14.

23. Claudia Wallis, "The Evolution Wars," *TIME*, August 15, 2005, 13.

24. Michael Behe in Claudia Wallis, "The Evolution Wars," *TIME*, August 15, 2005, 15.

25. Denyse O'Leary, *By Design or by Chance?* (Kitchener, ON: Castle Quay Books, 2004), 2.

26. Ibid., 16.

27. Ibid., 20.

28. Ibid., 3, 4, 11.

29. Stanley P. Wyatt, *Principles of Astronomy* (Boston: Allyn And Bacon, 1964), 523.

30. Claudia Wallis, "The Evolution Wars," *TIME*, August 15, 2005, 11, 14, 15; and Denyse O'Leary, By *Design or by Chance?* (Kitchener, ON: Castle Quay Books, 2004), 167 ff.

31. Michael J. Behe, *Darwin's Black Box: The Biochemical Challenge to Evolution* (New York: Free Press, 1996).

32. Denyse O'Leary, *By Design or by Chance?* (Kitchener, ON: Castle Quay Books, 2004), 44.

33. Claudia Wallis, "The Evolution Wars," *TIME*, August 15, 2005, 10.

34. Michael Behe in Claudia Wallis, "The Evolution Wars," *TIME*, August 15, 2005, 11.

35. Philip Yancey and Dr. Paul Brand, *Fearfully and Wonderfully Made* (Grand Rapids, MI: Zondervan, 1987), 122.

36. Ibid., 125.

37. Denyse O'Leary, *By Design or by Chance?* (Kitchener, ON: Castle Quay Books, 2004), 17.

38. James A. Beverley, Nelson's *Illustrated Guide to Religions* (Nashville: Thomas Nelson, 2009)

39. St. Augustine, *The Confessions of St. Augustine* (New York: Washington Square Press, 1962), section 8, 127–148.

40. Richard Dawkins, *The God Delusion* (New York: Houghton Mifflin, 2006), 97.

41. The Presbyterian Church in Canada, A *Statement of Christian Belief: Living Faith* (Winfield, BC: Wood Lake Books, 2000) 5.3.

42. Antony Flew, *The Philosophy of Religion* (London: Oxford University Press, 1971), 13 ff.

43. Ibid., 13.

44. Ibid., 14.

45. Richard Dawkins, *The God Delusion* (New York: Houghton Mifflin, 2006), 4.

46. Ibid., 94.

47. Ibid., 93.

48. F.F. Bruce, *The English Bible* (London: Methuen & Co, 1963), ix ff.

49. *The Westminster Confession of Faith* (Toronto: William Blackwood & Sons, MCMLVII), I.V.

50. John Calvin, *The Institutes of the Christian Faith* (London: James Clarke & Co, 1949), chapter V, 277 ff.

51. Thomas F. Torrance, *Theological Science* (London: Oxford University Press, 1969), 9 ff.

52. Karl Barth, *Church Dogmatics*, Vol. 1 (Edinburgh: T. & T. Clark, 1963), introduction, 1–2.

53. See http://www.wikipedia.org/wiki/Jesus_Seminar.

54. Tom Harpur, *The Pagan Christ* (Toronto: Thomas Allen Publishers, 2004), 67 ff.

55. The holy tomb and casket of an important Jewish king, believed to be that of King David, can be viewed in Jerusalem, just uphill from the Wailing Wall where the original foundation of the Temple of Solomon can be found. It is administered by the Jewish authorities and is open for viewing except on the Sabbath.

56. Pope Benedict XVI, *Jesus of Nazareth* (New York: Doubleday, 2007), 64 ff.

57. Ibid., 104–5.

58. Ibid., 104–5.

59. Ibid., 111.

60. These claims are found in John 9:5, John 6:35, John 11:25, John 14:6, and John 10:11.

61. Rodney Stark, *The Victory of Reason* (New York: Random House, 2005), 13 ff.

62.   Thomas F. Torrance, *Theological Science* (London: Oxford University Press, 1969).

63.   Rodney Stark, *The Victory of Reason* (New York: Random House, 2005), 11–12.

64.   Marcus J. Borg and, John D. Crossan, *The Last Week* (New York, Harperluxe, 2007).

65.   ABC television network, *Answering the Search for Jesus*, January 15, 2000.

66.   Harry Emerson Fosdick, *The Meaning of Prayer* (New York: Association Press, 1915).

67.   Harry Emerson Fosdick, *Dear Mr. Brown: Letters to a Person Perplexed about Religion* (New York: Harper & Brothers, 1961), chapter 13. Harry Emerson Fosdick, the founder of one of the largest Protestant church buildings in America on the edge of Columbia University in New York, was a noted preacher and prolific writer of many bestselling books. Fosdick was also known as the champion of the Modernist movement in America, taking many churches far left into a new liberalism.

68.   Adolf Harnack, *What Is Christianity* (London: Williams and Norgate, 1901), 63 ff.

69.   These kinds of statements appear in many of the extremely liberal religious thinkers, like the mid-twentieth century New Testament thinker, Rudolf Bultmann, and recently, Robert Funk.

70.   *The English Standard Version Study Bible* (Wheaton, IL: Crossway Bibles, 2008), 2213.

71.   Tom Harpur, *The Pagan Christ* (Toronto: Thomas Allen Publishers, 2004).

72.   Please see the notes in a good commentary. I recommend the notes found in *The English Standard Version Study Bible* (Wheaton, IL: Crossway Bibles, 2008), 2187–2191.

73. Frank Morison, *Who Moved The Stone?* (London: Faber and Faber, 1963), 11.

74. Ibid., 11.

75. Lee Strobel, *The Case For Easter* (Grand Rapids, MI: Zondervan, 2003), 7.

76. Ibid., 8.

77. Ibid., 5.

78. Ibid., 8.

79. Please see this account in Acts 17:16–34.

80. J.B. Phillips, *The Ring of Truth* (London: Hodder and Stoughton, 1967).

81. J.B. Phillips, *Your God is Too Small*, (London: The Epworth Press, 1962).

82. Billy Graham, *Just As I Am, The Autobiography Of Billy Graham* (Toronto: Harper Collins, 1997), 689.

83. *The Westminster Confession of Faith* (Toronto: William Blackwood & Sons, MCMLVII), XXXII.I.

84. Ibid., XXXII.II.

85. Alan Spraggett, "Column on Rabbi Abraham Feinberg," *The Toronto Star*, May 17, 1986, Religion Page, M1.

86. Ibid.

87. Ibid.

88. H.J. Schonfield, *The Passover Plot* (London: Hutchinson and Co, 1965).

89. The Presbyterian Church in Canada, *A Statement of Christian Belief: Living Faith* (Winfield, BC: Wood Lake Books, 2000) 10.2.

90. Bil Keane, "The Family Circus," *The Toronto Star*, June 6, 1986.

91. Lawrence Brice, *The Gamble of Faith* (Burlington, ON: Welch Publishing Company, 1989).

92. Aimee Dostoevsky, *Fyodor Dostoevsky: A Study*, in Ruth Bell Graham, *Prodigals and Those Who Love Them* (Grand Rapids, MI: Baker Books, 2008), 45–52.

93. God is raising up leaders in North America in the church, business, professional sports, and politics; in the founding of new Christian universities and the formation of new Christian television and radio programs and stations across North America; and, in Canada, in the establishment of a prestigious national newspaper, *The National Post*, that reports religious news accurately and fairly. The reality of a Christian renaissance of faith, a revival of biblical religion in North America, is building in many areas, not just among the elite, but also across much of our common culture.

COMING SPRING 2013

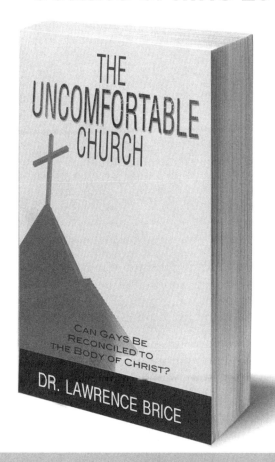

THE
UNCOMFORTABLE
CHURCH
CAN GAYS BE RECONCILED TO THE BODY OF CHRIST?

Rev. Dr. Lawrence Brice